THE ENTREPRENEUR'S

DRAGON ENERGY

THE MINDSET

KANYE, TRUMP,

AND YOU NEED TO SUCCEED

THE ENTREPRENEUR'S DRAGON ENERGY

978-0-9998649-6-8

The Entrepreneur's Dragon Energy
 ISBN: 978-0-9998649-6-8
 Copyright © 2019 by Clay Clark

Published by Thrive Publishing
 1100 Suite #100 Riverwalk Terrace
 Jenks, OK 74037

THE ENTREPRENEUR'S DRAGON ENERGY

SPECIAL DEDICATION

I dedicate this book to Vanessa Clark and Jonathan Kelly who have helped me harness and direct my "Dragon Energy" towards the achievement of positive causes and goals throughout the years. Thank you. I sincerely strive to fire up your lives without burning you.

TO MY KIDS

Scarlett and Aubrey, I'm glad that you were born with the "Dragon Energy," but mom and I will be helping you refine it so that you don't go to jail. Havana, Angelina, and Laya, I appreciate your patience and kindness, however, your mom and I will be working with you to develop your "Dragon Energy," so that the alphas of the world don't run over you.

TABLE OF CONTENTS

TABLE OF CONTENTS

INTRODUCTION:

If you aspire to dominate your industry and to become SUPER SUCCESSFUL, this book was written for you. This book will teach you how to discover and develop the relentlessness focus, commitment, and tenacity needed to succeed by harnessing your "Dragon Energy." Throughout my life, I have been blessed with the God-given air in my lungs and the mental capacity needed to build multiple multi-million dollar companies (www.EpicPhotos.com, www.DJConnection.com, www.MakeYourLifeEpic.com, Party Perfect—now known as Party Pro Rentals, etc), but I had to discover and learn how to harness the "Dragon Energy" to turn my "potential" and "talent" into actual skill and real results. This "Dragon Energy" is what gives me the force of will needed to passionately create the opportunities to interview many of the world's most successful people including:

» The New York Times best-selling co-author of Rich Dad Poor Dad, **Sharon Lechter**

» Senior editor for Forbes and best-selling author of 3 Kings, Michael Jackson Inc., and Empire State of Mind: How JAY-Z Went From Street Corner To Corner Office, **Zack O'Malley Greenburg**

» The founder and pastor of Life.Church—the largest Protestant church in America with over 100,000 weekly attendees—**Pastor Craig Groeschel**

» Creator of EOFire.com and the most downloaded business podcaster of all-time, **John Lee Dumas**

» The New York Times best-selling author of Purple Cow and former Yahoo! vice president of marketing, **Seth Godin**

» The New York Times best-selling author, award-winning podcaster, and Oprah guest, **Gretchen Rubin**

» Co-Founder of the 700+ employee advertising company AdRoll, **Adam Berke**

» Emmy award-winning producer of the Today Show and The New York Times best-selling author of Sh*tty Moms,
Mary Ann Zoellner

» The iconic inventor of several renowned products— SKYY Vodka, the Safetyglide hypodermic needle protector, a varicose vein stripper, the modern LED traffic light, a cryogenic cataract remover—and the holder of 50 patents for various consumer and medical products, **Maurice Kanbar**

» The founder of the billion-dollar chain of arts and crafts stores, Hobby Lobby, **David Green**

» The New York Times best-selling author of Contagious: Why Things Catch On and Wharton Business School professor, **Jonah Berger**

» The New York Times best-selling author of Made to Stick and Duke University professor, **Dan Heath**

» International best-selling author of In Search of Excellence, **Tom Peters**

» NBA player and coach, and the shortest player to ever play in the league, **Muggsy Bogues**

» The New York Times best-selling author and business case study expert, **Jason Jennings**

» NFL running back and winner of Dancing with the Stars, **Rashad Jennings**

» NBA Hall of Famer, two-time NBA Champion, and two-time Olympic Gold Medalist, **David Robinson**

» The former executive vice president of Walt Disney World who once managed 40,000 employees, **Lee Cockerell**

» The New York Times best-selling author, blind and successful entrepreneur and Emmy award winner, **Jim Stovall**

THE ENTREPRENEUR'S DRAGON ENERGY

» **Michael Levine**, the PR consultant of choice for Michael Jackson, Prince, Nike, Charlton Heston, Nancy Kerrigan, and others

» The president and CEO of the billion-dollar convenience store chain QuikTrip, **Chet Cadieux**

» **Johnny G**, the inventor of the spin class phenomenon, Spinning®

» **Wes Carter**, the attorney for TD Jakes and Joyce Meyers

» **Paul Pressey**, 10-year NBA player, 20+ year NBA assistant coach for the Los Angeles Lakers, the Orlando Magic, the Boston Celtics, and others

» **Rachel Faucett**, the social media advisor of choice for Disney, Pottery Barn, and Hobby Lobby

» **Jill Donovan**, "Mom-Preneur" and retail product developer whose Rustic Cuff products have been worn by Oprah, Britney Spears, and countless celebrities

» The best-selling author of Search Engine for Dummies, **Bruce Clay**

» Billboard contemporary chart-topping singer-songwriter and Atlantic Records recording artist, **Colton Dixon**

» Grammy Award winner, former manager of 2 Chainz, Nike athlete, and commercial star, **Charlie "Rocket" Jabaley**

» Conservative talk pundit, frequent Fox News contributor, political commentator, and best-selling author, **Ben Shapiro**

» And countless other entrepreneurial success stories

Throughout my life I have been sexually abused; my best-friend and roommate died in a car accident during college; my wife and I had a son who was born blind; as a married couple we've experienced miscarriages; my Dad died of ALS (Lou Gehrig's Disease); I've been screwed over by former employees; and I have gone through every possible form of non-compete violations and trust-violating friendship betrayal, but I refuse to be a victim. I refuse to lose.

I can assure you from first-hand experience, that this is something I share with all of the SUPER SUCCESSFUL PEOPLE who I have interviewed. What do Kanye West and President Donald Trump have in common? They SHARE ALMOST THE EXACT SAME MINDSET and WORLD VIEW in spite of their religious or political affiliations. Kanye West refers to this as "Dragon Energy." The vast majority of people don't understand this "Dragon Energy," and therefore easily dismiss Kanye West and President Donald Trump's affection for each other as mere headline hunting and a publicity pursuit. I love it, I enjoy it, I understand it, I have it, I celebrate it, and I teach it. This "Dragon Energy" mindset is what has allowed me to beat the crap out of my competitors consistently for 22 years now (as a self-employed man who just now turned 38). So now without any further ado, here is the tweet that inspired me to write this book:

> **ye** ✓
> @kanyewest
>
> You don't have to agree with trump but the mob can't make me not love him. We are both dragon energy. He is my brother. I love everyone. I don't agree with everything anyone does. That's what makes us individuals. And we have the right to independent thought.
>
> ♡ 326K   10:30 AM - Apr 25, 2018
>
> 💬 107K people are talking about this

The president of the United States, Donald J. Trump, then responded to Kanye and thanked him for his outspoken support of his polarizing Presidency:

Kanye's wife, the unofficial president and princess of the tabloids and celebrity fame, Kim Kardashian, then tweeted the following statement:

My friends, the 21-time Grammy Award winner has said on record, "President Bush doesn't care about black people." But, even though President Trump is an outspoken, wall-building proponent whose conservative political views clash with nearly all of the left-leaning celebrities, the shared respect that President Trump and Kanye West have for each other is transcendent because it is based on their shared "Dragon Energy." President Trump, Kanye West, and all super successful people share a relentless work ethic and an unparalleled commitment to be the best in the world at whatever they are passionately pursuing at the time.

Throughout the careers of Kanye West's and Donald Trump they have had undeniable success in a variety of industries as a result of their ability to harness their "Dragon Energy." Regardless of whether we like their politics, their music or their personalities, Kanye West and Donald Trump have changed the landscape of entire industries. They each have made millions of dollars for themselves, billions of dollars for the economy, and have created thousands of jobs. None of this would be possible without this "Dragon Energy."

If you are sincerely seeking to understand the actual, real and raw mindsets of super successful people then you will love this book.

If you are an easily offended and a rejection-averse human pretender who loves to focus on your feelings and high-brow theories or if you enjoy watching endless reruns of TED Talk videos to avoid actually getting to work, then you should not read this book because we are going to irritate each other. You will irritate me because you are wrong and poor because of it, and I will irritate you because I am right and therefore successful.

NOTABLE QUOTABLE

"My observation is that the doers are the major thinkers. The people that really create the things that change the industry are both the thinker-doer in the same person. Leonardo was the artist but he also mixed his own paints, he also was a fairly good chemist, knew about pigments, knew about human anatomy. Combining all of those skills together, the art and the science, the thinking and the doing, resulted in the exceptional result. And there is no difference in our industry – the people that have really made the contributions have been the thinkers and the doers."

- Steve Jobs (The co-founder of Apple, the founder of NeXT, and the former CEO of PIXAR)

THE ENTREPRENEUR'S DRAGON ENERGY

This book is filled with countless, counter-cultural, game-changing knowledge bombs, but it will be an epic waste of time for both of us if you do not aggressively take notes as you read about and wrestle with the harsh realities of how life works and how super successful people proactively create themselves, their lives and their wealth. These concepts are rarely taught by teachers on college campuses or high schools because the vast majority of teachers have a poverty mindset and the strong belief that the world should pay them based upon the hours they work and not for the value they add to each hour. People who have the "Dragon Energy" are different than most people, they are eccentric and they earn dramatically more than everybody else.

NOTABLE QUOTABLE

"My passionate sense of social justice and social responsibility has always contrasted oddly with my pronounced lack of need for direct contact with other human beings and human communities. I am truly a 'lone traveler' and have never belonged to my country, my home, my friends, or even my immediate family, with my whole heart; in the face of all these ties, I have never lost a sense of distance and a need for solitude..."

- Albert Einstein (The German-born physicist who first suggested to the United States during World War II that we should get started on creating a nuclear bomb or we would all be speaking German.)

**Below is the letter written by the theoretical physicist, Albert Einstein (who most thought to be half-crazy) to President Franklin Delano Roosevelt. This saved America from certain destruction at the hands of the Nazi atomic bomb program. At the time that Albert Einstein wrote this letter, the United States had yet to create an atomic bomb because we allowed the bureaucrats without the "Dragon Energy" to be put in charge of our weapons creation program.

F.D. Roosevelt
President of the United States
White House
Washington, D.C.

Sir:

Some recent work by E. Fermi and L. Szilard, which has been communicated to me in manuscript, leads me to expect that the element uranium may be turned into a new and important source of energy in the immediate future. Certain aspects of the situation which has arisen seem to call for watchfulness and if necessary, quick action on the part of the Administration. I believe therefore that it is my duty to bring to your attention the following facts and recommendations.

In the course of the last four months it has been made probable through the work of Joliot in France as well as Fermi and Szilard in America—that it may be possible to set up a nuclear chain reaction in a large mass of uranium, by which vast amounts of power and large quantities of new radium-like elements would be generated. Now it appears almost certain that this could be achieved in the immediate future.

This new phenomenon would also lead to the construction of bombs, and it is conceivable—though much less certain—that extremely powerful bombs of this type may thus be constructed. A single bomb of this type, carried by boat and exploded in a port, might very well destroy the whole port together with some of the surrounding territory. However, such bombs might very well prove too heavy for transportation by air.

The United States has only very poor ores of uranium in moderate quantities. There is some good ore in Canada and former Czechoslovakia, while the most important source of uranium is in the Belgian Congo.

In view of this situation you may think it desirable to have some permanent contact maintained between the Administration and the group of physicists working on chain reactions in America. One possible way of achieving this might be for you to entrust the task with a person who has your confidence and who could perhaps serve in an unofficial capacity. His task might comprise the following:

a) to approach Government Departments, keep them informed of the further development, and put forward recommendations for Government action, giving particular attention to the problem of securing a supply of uranium ore for the United States.

b) to speed up the experimental work, which is at present being carried on within the limits of the budgets of University laboratories, by providing funds, if such funds be required, through his contacts with private persons who are willing to make contributions for this cause, and perhaps also by obtaining co-operation of industrial laboratories which have necessary equipment.

I understand that Germany has actually stopped the sale of uranium from the Czechoslovakian mines which she has taken over. That she should have taken such early action might perhaps be understood on the ground that the son of the German Under-Secretary of State, von Weizsacker, is attached to the Kaiser-Wilhelm Institute in Berlin, where some of the American work on uranium is now being repeated.

A. Einstein

Albert Einstein

WHY KANYE WEST AND PRESIDENT DONALD TRUMP ARE CULTURALLY RELEVANT

KANYE WEST SUCCESS 101:

Kanye West is an American artist married to the omnipresent tabloid princess, Kim Kardashian, and who has achieved success in multiple industries including:

» Music production

» Music video directing

» Rapping

» Fashion design

» Songwriting

HIS HISTORY:

» 1977 - On June 8th, Kanye Omari West was born in Atlanta, Georgia.

» 1977 - Kanye's father, Ray, was a photojournalist who was politically active with the Black Panthers and later went on to become a Christian counselor.

» 1980 - Age 3 - Kanye's parents divorced when he was just three years old. From that point forward, Kanye was raised in the middle-class area of Chicago known as South Shore.

» 1987 - Age 10 - Kanye and his mom moved to China where his mom taught as part of an exchange program with a university.

» 1988 - Age 8 - When Kanye returned to Chicago, he developed a magnificent obsession for South Side Chicago's hip hop scene and became friends with a DJ and producer by the name of No I.D.

» 1995 - Age 18 - Kanye graduated from Polaris High School and went on to win a scholarship to study at Chicago's American Academy of Art. However, he wisely decided to drop out of college to pursue his career in the world of music.

» 1996–2002 - Age 19–24 - Kanye West devoted thousands of hours to creating beats and tracks for local artists and eventually developed a signature style known as "chipmunk soul," which was known to feature soul music samples that were sped up to sound like "chipmunks."

» 2001 - Age 24 - Without any connections and any knowledge of how he was going to break into the hip hop and rap music scene, he boldly moved to New York in 2001.

» 2001 - Age 24 - Kanye West secured his first big break as a result of his relentless marketing, and was charged with handling the production for a JAY-Z song called, "This Can't Be Life," which was used on JAY-Z's 2000 album, Dynasty: Roc La Familia. Kanye then went on to produce incredible beats for household names in the world of hip hop and R&B including: Mos Def, Talib Kweli, Ludacris, Alicia Keys, John Legend, Beyonce, Beanie Sigel, Goodie Mob, Jermaine Dupri, Foxy Brown, Nas, DMX, Nappy Roots, Fabolous, Janet Jackson, Carl Thomas, The Game, Common, Britney Spears, Mariah Carey, T.I., Lupe Fiasco, Michael Jackson, Drake, Rick Ross,

Snoop Dogg, Justin Bieber, 2 Chainz, Rihanna, Big Sean, Christina Aguilera, and others.

» 2002 - Age 25 - Kanye West produced four songs on JAY-Z's album, The Blueprint, which many consider to be one of the greatest rap albums of all time.

» 2004 - Age 27 - Kanye West decided to transition to become an actual recording artist himself despite countless rejections from JAY-Z and others. During 2004 he also won the best New Male Artist at both the 2004 World Music Awards and 2004 Billboard Music Awards.

West's debut album, The College Dropout, which won several awards and secured Kanye West with ten nominations at the 47th Annual Grammy Awards. The album and its single, "Jesus Walks," won Best Rap Album and Best Rap Song at the ceremony.

» 2005 - Age 28 - He earned the MTV Video Music Award for Best Male Video at the 2005 MTV Video Music Awards. West also released his second studio album which he received eight Grammy nominations for at the 48th Annual Grammy Awards.

» 2007 - Age 30 - Kanye's mother was a school teacher who went on to become a professor of English at Chicago State University. She was her son's manager until she passed away at the age of just 58 as a result of heart disease after receiving cosmetic surgery in 2007.

» 2007 - Age 30 - Kanye West received eight additional awards at the 50th Annual Grammy Awards for his third studio album, Graduation. He ultimately won four out of the five rap categories and became the first solo artist to have three studio albums to be nominated for a Grammy.

» 2008 - Age 31 - West released his fourth studio album, 808s & Heartbreak, in 2008 which was nominated for the Album of the Year at the 2009 Soul Train Music Awards. The featured single, "Love Lockdown," received three nominations at the 2009 MTV Video Music

Awards, including Video of the Year. Also in 2009, Kanye West won a record-equalling third Brit Award for International Male Solo Artist.

» 2010 - Age 33 - West's fifth studio album My Beautiful Dark Twisted Fantasy (2010) and collaborative album Watch The Throne (2011) with JAY-Z earned him the most nominations at the 54th Annual Grammy Awards—seven, of which he won four. He repeated the feat a year later, when he led (jointly) the Grammy nominees for a fifth time at the 55th Annual Grammy Awards, taking home three awards.

» 2016 - Age 39 - In 2016, Kanye West and Adidas made history with their new game-changing partnership which was the most significant partnership ever between an athletic brand and a non-athlete.

» FUN FACT: "One hour after the Boost 350 sneakers went on sale for $200, for example, they were sold out in stores and online." —Kanye West's secret to building a footwear empire to compete with Nike - https://www.businessinsider.com/how-kanye-west-made-yeezy-brand-a-success-2018-4

» Throughout his career, he's been named by Time Magazine in the 100 Most Influential People List twice.

» 2016 - Kanye had an epic meltdown on stage and was hospitalized and he later cancelled the rest of his tour.

» 2018 - During an interview that recorded with radio host, Big Boy, Kanye shared that he was first diagnosed with a "mental disorder" when was 39 years old. However, he went on to say, "But like I said on the album. It's not a disability, it's a super power."

WHY KANYE WESTAND PRESIDENT DONALD TRUMP ARE CULTURALLY RELEVANT

DONALD TRUMP SUCCESS 101:

Donald John Trump was born on June 14th 1946 and was elected as the 45th and current president of the United States. Before he decided to enter the world of politics, he built his fortune in the real estate, entertainment, self-help, and television industries.

HIS HISTORY:

FUN FACTS:

Who is Donald Trump? According to a 2017 Forbes estimate, Donald Trump's net worth is approximately $3.1 billion.

$1.6 billion is in New York real estate

$570 million is in golf clubs and resorts

$500 million is in non-New York real estate

$290 million is in cash and personal assets

$200 million is in brand businesses

**According to Fortune magazine, his net worth has gone down from $3.7 billion to $3.1 billion because of the overall declining value of New York real estate.

In 2017 he dropped to number 248 in the ranks for the richest people in America according to Forbes. He's down from his ranking as the 156th richest person in America in 2016.

FUN FACT:

President Donald J. Trump is the best-selling author of several books including:

The Art of the Deal (1987)

The Art of the Comeback (1997)

Why We Want You to Be Rich (2006)

Trump 101: The Way to Success (2006)

Trump Never Give Up: How I Turned My Biggest Challenges into Success (2008)

NOTABLE QUOTABLE

"Until several months ago, I would have said not all that different. He was then and is now always 100 percent self-absorbed, incapable of interest in other human beings, and completely self-referential. He viewed every event through the lens of its impact on him. Even 30 years ago, he had an incredibly short attention span. Lying was almost second nature to him; he did it as easily as most of us drink a glass of water. All of those things have turned out to be very similar all throughout his life, and he himself has said, 'I'm pretty much the same person at 70 that I was at 7.' I believe that's true."

- Tony Schwartz, The Nation interview - https://www. thenation.com/article/donald-trumps-ghostwriter-says-the-president-is-now-in-survival-mode/

FUN FACT:

Howard Kaminsky was a book publisher who died at the age of 77 and was the publisher of Donald Trump's first book, The Art of the Deal. Howard

said that Donald Trump did not play a role in the writing of his own book. Howard told The New Yorker, "Trump didn't write a postcard for us!"

- https://www.usnews.com/news/articles/2016-07-18/ behind-the-art-of-the-deal-trumps-ghostwriter- calls-candidate-a-sociopath

He has been married to three different women:

» Wife #1 - Ivana Trump (1977–1992)
  A Czech-American businesswoman, former fashion model, author, and television personality. She was the first wife of Donald Trump from 1977 until 1992.

» Wife #2 - Marla Maples (1993–1999)
  An American actress, television personality, and Donald Trump's second wife (1993-99).

» Wife #3 - Melania Knauss (January 22, 2005)
  The First Lady of the United States and third wife of the 45th president of the United States, Donald Trump. She was born in Novo Mesto, Slovenia on April 26, 1970 (Donald Trump was born on June 14, 1946). Melania grew up in Sevnica, Lower Sava Valley. She worked as a fashion model for agencies in Milan and Paris, and later moved to New York City in 1996. She initially worked in the United States prior to receiving a legal work visa. Her modeling career was associated with Irene Marie Models and Trump Model Management. In 2001, she obtained a green card and became a lawful permanent resident of the United States. She married Donald Trump in 2005 and obtained U.S. citizenship in 2006. She is the first naturalized U.S. citizen to become First Lady of the United States.

THE TIMELINE OF DONALD TRUMP

» 1927 (19 years Pre-Donald) - Donald's father (Fred Trump) began his career by working in construction and sales. He created a company by the name of E. Trump & Son in 1927.

He grew this business to the point where he actually owned and controlled an estimated 27,000 apartments within New York City. He owned single family homes in Queens and apartments for the U.S. Navy personnel located near the major shipyards on the east coast.

» 1946 - Donald Trump was born in Queens, New York on June 14th.

» 1958 - Age 12 - Donald Trump attended Kew-Forest School in Forest Hills, Queens where his father served on the governing board.

» 1959 - Age 13 - Donald kept getting himself into a lot of trouble so his father Fred sent him off to the New York Military Academy to get his life together and to learn some discipline.

NOTABLE QUOTABLE

"As an adolescent, I was mostly interested in creating mischief,"

- President Donald J. Trump (The 45th President of the United States, Successful Businessman, Television Personality, Owner of Miss USA and Miss Universe pageants and Co-Author of "The Art of The Deal")

NOTABLE QUOTABLE

"Without passion you don't have energy, without energy you have nothing."

- Donald Trump

» 1962 - Age 15 - He began working for his father's company, E. Trump & Son.

» 1964 - Age 17 - He graduated from the New York Military Academy.

THE ENTREPRENEUR'S DRAGON ENERGY

» 1964 - Age 17 - He attended Fordham College at Rose Hill for two years. Trump originally wanted to become a movie producer, but he was denied by the University of Southern California when he applied to go there.

» 1964 - Age 17 - His father bought the Swifton Village apartment complex that was 50% vacant—but the largest apartment complex—at a foreclosure auction. Donald Trump was a senior in high school at the military academy when his dad bought the complex, but he played a big role in managing the project while going through both high school and college.

» 1966 - Age 19 - He transferred to Penn's Wharton School of Business and began buying properties in Philadelphia almost immediately.

What did Donald Trump do while at Wharton?

class. He was not known on campus for any reason at all,' his Wharton classmate Nancy Hano told The Daily News. Another classmate, Stanton Koppel, told the publication, 'I have no memory of him whatsoever.'"

—*Fortune Magazine - http://fortune. com/2015/08/14/donald-trump-wharton*

FUN FACT:

"Writing in The New York Times magazine in 1984, William Geist reported that 'the commencement program from 1968 does not list him as graduating with honors of any kind,' even though 'just about every profile ever written about Mr. Trump states that he graduated first in his class at Wharton in 1968.'"

- *http://fortune.com/2015/08/14/donald-trump-wharton*

> » 1968 - Age 22 - He graduated from the University of Pennsylvania in 1968 with a bachelor's degree.

NOTABLE QUOTABLE

"What separates the winners from the losers is how a person reacts to each new twist of fate."

- *President Donald J. Trump*

FUN FACT:

A 1968 commencement program shared by The Daily Pennsylvanian backs that up. It shows that Trump graduated from the undergraduate school of finance and commerce, but he did not graduate at the top of his class or with honors.

- *http://www.pennlive.com/news/2017/02/what_is_ trumps_real_record_at.html*

THE ENTREPRENEUR'S DRAGON ENERGY

NOTABLE QUOTABLE

"He got his start when he turned a big profit on a Cincinnati apartment complex his father assigned him after his Wharton graduation in 1968."

- https://www.wharton.upenn.edu/wp-content/ uploads/125anniversaryissue/trump.html

FUN FACT:

Before Donald Trump became a household name, wrote best-selling books, became a reality TV star, and became the billionaire president of the United States, he had to start somewhere. Donald learned real estate as a result of working for his father's construction company managing apartments.

NOTABLE QUOTABLE

"Hunt for bargains. Chase out deadbeats. Spend some money on paint and polish."

- Fred Trump, Donald's father - http://beta. latimes.com/politics/la-na-pol-donald-trump-housing-20160815-snap-story.html

FUN FACT:

Donald Trump's father was one of the biggest landlords in New York at one time, owning 39 buildings and 14,000 units mostly located in Queens and Brooklyn.

NOTABLE QUOTABLE

"You have to think anyway, so why not think big?"

- President Donald J. Trump

» 1971 - Age 24 - After proving to himself and to his father that he could effectively manage and turn-around the largest apartment complex in Cincinnati at the age of 21, he asked his father if he could get involved in massive building projects in Manhattan.

» 1972 - Age 25 - Trump became the owner of E. Trump & Son and renamed it The Trump Organization.

» 1973 - Age 26 - While serving as the president of the Trump Organization, Donald was responsible for overseeing and managing 14,000 apartments across Brooklyn, Queens, and Staten Island.

ASK YOURSELF:

» If you had to manage 14,000 units of anything, how would you handle it?

» If you had to manage 14,000 humans, how would you manage your time?

» 1973 - Age 26 - The United States Justice Department sued the Trump Organization, charging that it frequently violated the Fair Housing Act by discriminating against black potential buyers.

In October 1973, the Justice Department filed a civil rights case accusing the Trump firm, whose complexes contained 14,000 apartments, of violating the Fair Housing Act of 1968.

The Trumps retained Roy Cohn, a defense attorney who had been a top aide to the Republican Senator Joseph during his infamous effort to root out communists in government. Cohn portrayed the Trumps as the victims and counter-sued the government, demanding it pay them $100 million for falsely accusing them of discrimination." - https://www.washingtonpost.com/politics/inside-the-governments-racial-bias-case-against-donald-trumps-company-and-how-he-fought-it/2016/01/23/fb90163e-bfbe-11e5-bcda-62a36b394160_story.html?utm_term=.746491cf7ee1

THE ENTREPRENEUR'S DRAGON ENERGY

ASK YOURSELF:

» At the age of 26 how would you deal with a lawsuit being brought against you by the Justice Department?

» 1978 - Age 32 - The city of New York selected one of the pieces of land owned by Donald Trump on the West Side of Manhattan to be the location of the Jacob Javits Convention Center. Trump received a broker's fee for selling the property.

» 1978 - Age 32 - Donald decided to take on the massively ambitious project of attempting to renovate the failing Commodore Hotel. The building was in disrepair and in massive need of total overhaul. The city of New York was littered with crime, drugs, and litter at the time. He replaced the worn out brick facade with glass and replaced the existing lobby with a massive atrium. When the project opened in September of 1980, it put Donald Trump on the map and in the public eye. Fred provided a $1 million loan from Fred Trump's Village Construction Corp. Fred and the Hyatt Hotel also guaranteed the $70 million construction loan.

Donald negotiated a 40-year tax abatement for the hotel with the city in exchange for a share of the venture's profits. The deal helped reduce the risk of the project and provided an incentive for investors to participate.

» 1979 - Age 33 - While still renovating The Commodore Hotel, Trump began construction of Trump Tower, the tower that now serves as the headquarters of The Trump Organization.

NOTABLE QUOTABLE

"No dream is too big. No challenge is too great. Nothing we want for our future is beyond our reach."

- President Donald J. Trump

» 1980 - Age 34 - Trump finished remodeling the Hyatt Hotel (the former Commodore Hotel). The hotel was reopened on September 25th, 1980. The Governor of New York at the time, Hugh Carey, and the Mayor of New York, Ed Koch, were both in attendance for the grand opening.

» 1980 - The rink was closed in 1980 for a proposed two years of renovations at $9.1 million. Six years after the problem-plagued work was still not completed by the city, Donald Trump persuaded Mayor Ed Koch to let him complete the work in four months at $3 million in order to have it open by the end of the year. Koch initially objected but later agreed. Trump finished the job in the promised four months at a final cost 25% below the budget and for no profit.

» 1981 - Age 35 - Trump purchased and renovated a building that would become the Trump Plaza on Third Avenue in New York City. Trump made this into an apartment cooperative, in which tenants partly owned the building.

» 1982 - Age 36 - Mayor Ed Koch and Donald Trump celebrated the completion of Trump Tower in Manhattan.

THE ENTREPRENEUR'S DRAGON ENERGY

» 1983 - Age 37 - Grand opening of Trump Tower in Manhattan.

» 1983 - Age 37 - Trump finished the completion of his 58-story skyscraper known as the Trump Tower.

NOTABLE QUOTABLE

"It's tangible, it's solid, it's beautiful. It's artistic, from my standpoint, and I just love real estate."

- President Donald J. Trump

The New York Times wrote, "That Mr. Trump was able to obtain the location ... is testimony to [his] persistence and to his skills as a negotiator."

The tower is a 58-story, 664-foot-high (202 m) mixed-use skyscraper.

It's located at 721–725 Fifth Avenue between 56th and 57th Streets in Midtown Manhattan, New York City.

The building is located in one of midtown Manhattan's special zoning districts, but Trump was able to get the tower approved because it was a mixed-use development.

He was able to get it approved to be so tall as a result of building a massive atrium on the ground floor.

FUN FACT:

Trump considers 725 5th Avenue his home.

FUN FACT:

There are 263 apartments in the building.

FUN FACT:

Michael Jackson rented a condominium
in the building during the 1990s.

FUN FACT:

The building was where the famous reality
show The Apprentice was filmed.

FUN FACT:

The public space includes a coffee shop, an ice
cream store, an apparel store, and a restaurant.

NOTABLE QUOTABLE

"Success is going from failure to failure
without losing enthusiasm."

—*Winston Churchill, Prime Minister of the United
Kingdom from 1940 to 1945 and again from 1951 to 1955*

» 1984 - Age 38 - FAIL - Trump Buys the New Jersey
Generals

Trump's football adventure began in 1984, when he
bought the New Jersey Generals, part of the then-
new United States Football League. The USFL, as
chronicled in an excellent installment of ESPN's 30 for
30 series, was envisioned by founder David Dixon as a
complement to the National Football League that would
play in the spring, leaving fall to the NFL. For its first
three years the strategy seemed successful.

But it wasn't enough for Trump. He pushed hard to shift
the USFL to a fall schedule, where the USFL—with less
talent and less public awareness—would go head-to-
head with the bigger league.

The decision to switch to fall play immediately crippled several USFL teams, who wouldn't be able to compete directly with local NFL teams. The league even turned down a lifeline in the form of lucrative TV offers to broadcast spring games.

But Trump's plan was typically audacious and risky. Rather than organically grow a new league, he hoped to force an immediate merger with the NFL, which would provide huge returns for surviving USFL team owners. That goal hinged in part on an antitrust lawsuit alleging the NFL was an unlawful monopoly.

But things didn't go Trump's way. While the USFL technically won the antitrust case, the jury concluded mismanagement was mostly at fault for its problems. There was no merger and no buyouts. By 1986, the USFL was finished.

» 1985 - Age 38 - Donald J. Trump, purchased cereal heiress Marjorie Merriweather Post's landmark Mar-a-Lago estate. After years of fighting with the town of Palm Beach, he was finally allowed him to convert the historic property into a private club.

» 1986 - Age 39 - Trump Place - The residential complex initially intended to become "Television City" opened on the West Side after Trump's television dreams were crushed.

"He planned to build a $4.5 billion project called Television City, later Trump City. It would have included 5,700 apartments and a 150-story skyscraper that would have been the world's largest, had Trump not quickly abandoned that plan. He had also hoped the complex would become NBC's new headquarters. To make the numbers work, he needed a $700 million property tax abatement, but Mayor Edward Koch wouldn't give it to him. Trump waged a public relations war, saying Koch had 'no talent and only moderate intelligence.'

Koch called Trump 'piggy, piggy, piggy,' then granted NBC tax incentives to stay in Rockefeller Center, as Trump chronicler Tim O'Brien wrote at Bloomberg View. In 1994, Trump defaulted on about $1 billion in loans for the project and had to sell a majority stake to Hong Kong investors, who built the condo complex now called Riverside South, paying Trump a fee to put his name on some buildings. In 2005, the Asian owners sold the whole thing for $1.8 billion to private equity giant Carlyle Group and Extell Development Corp., run by Gary Barnett. Trump, who retained about a 30% interest, sued, arguing he could have sold it for more. But, ultimately, he failed to block the sale. Trump's profit: About $425 million." - http://www.businessinsider.com/3-major-trump-real-estate-failures-2016-4

» 1986 - Age 40 - Trump purchased the twin-tower Plaza condominium buildings in West Palm Beach for $40 million in a foreclosure sale and installed a sign that said "Trump Plaza" in five foot high letters atop each of the buildings.

» 1987 - Age 41 - Trump released the smash hit and The New York Times best-selling book, The Art of the Deal.

FUN FACT:

The Art of the Deal (1987) - It was the first book published by Trump, and helped to make him a household name. It reached number one on The New York Times Best-Seller list, stayed there for 13 weeks, and altogether held a position on the list for 48 weeks.

» 1988 - Age 41 - March 27th - Donald Trump bought The Plaza Hotel.

THE ENTREPRENEUR'S DRAGON ENERGY

He said in an interview that his wife, Ivanka, would become president of the Plaza - with a salary of '$1 a year plus all the dresses she can buy.' Unlike most of his other properties, which carry the Trump name, the Plaza will remain the Plaza.

"It's got the most important name in the world, and it's going to remain that way,' he [President Donald Trump] said." - http://www.nytimes.com/1988/03/27/nyregion/plaza-hotel-is-sold-to-donald-trump-for-390-million.html

---

NOTABLE QUOTABLE

"Brand is just a perception, and perception will match reality over time. Sometimes it will be ahead, other times it will be behind. But brand is simply a collective impression some have about a product."

- Elon Musk (The iconic entrepreneur, investor, and engineer behind Tesla, SpaceX, PayPal, SolarCity, Neuralink, and more.)

ASK YOURSELF:

How highly would you rank your brand and business in the following areas on a scale of 1 to 10 with 10 being the highest?

» Your personal appearance
1 2 3 4 5 6 7 8 9 10

» Your communication skills
1 2 3 4 5 6 7 8 9 10

» Your business cards
1 2 3 4 5 6 7 8 9 10

» Your website
1 2 3 4 5 6 7 8 9 10

» Your print materials
1 2 3 4 5 6 7 8 9 10

» Your billboards
1 2 3 4 5 6 7 8 9 10

» Your one sheets
1 2 3 4 5 6 7 8 9 10

» Your online advertisements
1 2 3 4 5 6 7 8 9 10

» 1988–1992 - Age 41–45 - FAIL - Trump Airlines

Trump took out a $245 million loan to purchase the planes of Eastern Air Shuttle. Trump's vision was to rebrand the blue-collar airline as a premium and upscale airline. Two years into the business, it was not making enough money to cover the monthly $1,000,000 interest payment and Trump turned the business over to his creditors.

During his period of financial difficulties in 1991, the airline was taken over by USAir, and Trump's Trump Taj Mahal casino in Atlantic City declared bankruptcy. Two other casinos owned by Trump, as well as his Plaza Hotel in New York City, went bankrupt in 1992. Estimates of his net worth during that period ranged from zero to $2 billion.

» 1989 - Age 42 - January - Trump appeared on the cover of Time Magazine. - http://content.time.com/time/covers/0,16641,19890116,00.html

THE ENTREPRENEUR'S DRAGON ENERGY

FUN FACT:

Headline - "This man may turn you green with envy, or just turn you off. Flaunting it is the game and TRUMP is the name."

- Time Magazine - January of 1989

» 1989 - Age 42 - The book, Trump the Game, was mass-produced.

» 1989 - FUN FACT: "Five people, including three high-level executives of Donald J. Trump's three casinos in Atlantic City, were killed yesterday when their helicopter crashed in pine woodlands on the Garden State Parkway near Forked River, N.J." - http://www.nytimes.com/1989/10/11/nyregion/copter-crash-kills-3-aides-of-trump.html

» 1991 - Age 44 - FAIL - Bankruptcy #1 - Trump Taj Mahal Casino

FUN FACT:

"The Trump Taj Mahal, the Atlantic City, N.J., casino that the real estate mogul built for $1.2 billion in 1990, went for 4 cents on the dollar when it was sold in March."

— https://www.latimes.com/business/la-fi-trump-taj-mahal-20170509-story.html

FUN FACT:

Trump has filed for bankruptcy four times.

DEFINITION - What is "Bankruptcy"?

"Bankruptcy is a legal proceeding involving a person or business that is unable to repay outstanding debts. The bankruptcy process begins with a petition filed by the debtor, which is most common, or on behalf of creditors, which is less common. All of the debtor's assets are measured and evaluated, and the assets may be used to repay a portion of outstanding debt."

——Investopedia

DEFINITION - Chapter 11 Bankruptcy -

A form of bankruptcy that involves a reorganization of a debtor's business affairs, debts and assets. Named after the U.S. bankruptcy code 11, Chapter 11 is generally filed by corporations that require time to restructure their debts and gives the debtor a fresh start, subject to the debtor's fulfillment of his obligations under the plan of reorganization. As the most complex of all bankruptcy cases and generally the most expensive, a company should consider Chapter 11 reorganization only after careful analysis and exploration of all other alternatives. They paid $50 million for it. The hotel, which Trump called "the 8th wonder of the world" back in the 1990s, cost $1.2 billion to build.

» 1991 - Age 44 - Trump relinquished the 33-story Trump Plaza condo towers in West Palm Beach to lenders after borrowing $60 million to complete the project. However, his name remains atop the structures.

» 1992 - Age 45 - Three Casinos—the Taj Mahal, the Castle, and the Plaza went bankrupt.

» 1992 - Age 45 - FAIL - Bankruptcy #2 - Trump Castle Associates

He had to give up half of his ownership in the Plaza Hotel. Trump's Castle owned Trump Taj Mahal, Atlantic City's third-largest casino, which had 70,000 square feet of casino space and 725 rooms.

» 1995 - Age 48 - Trump bought the 40th Wall Street Tower for $8 million dollars, and according to Bloomberg, this tower is now worth $550 million.

PRESS CLIPPINGS - The real estate developer Donald J. Trump completed his purchase of 40 Wall Street yesterday, buying the distinguished 70-story office building, across the street from the New York

THE ENTREPRENEUR'S DRAGON ENERGY

Stock Exchange, for a price estimated at less than $8 million.

Mr. Trump in July had disclosed an agreement to buy the building, which contains 1.1 million square feet of space, from Kinson Properties of Hong Kong. Kinson paid $8 million for it in 1993.

While representatives of Mr. Trump declined to disclose the price he had paid, published reports said it was less than $8 million.

In July, representatives of the developer said he planned to spend $100 million converting the building, which is 89 percent vacant, to more modern offices.

> » 1996 - Age 49 - Trump bought the Miss Universe Organization. In 1996, he partnered with NBC to purchase the Miss Universe Organization, which produces the Miss America, Miss USA, and Miss Teen USA beauty pageants.

NOTABLE QUOTABLE

During a 2005 appearance on Howard Stern's show, Trump bragged about being able to go backstage to women getting dressed. "I'll go backstage before a show, and everyone's getting dressed and ready and everything else."

- President Donald J. Trump

> » 1997 - Age 50 - Trump broke ground on construction of the Trump International Golf Club, a $40 million course just south of Palm Beach International Airport. It was completed in 2000.

NOTABLE QUOTABLE

"The beauty of me is that I'm very rich."

- *President Donald J. Trump*

FUN FACT:

According to a Vanity Fair article, the Club's initial fee is $100,000, and the 500 exclusive members must pay $14,000 in annual dues to remain members.

» 1999 - Age 53 - Trump established Trump Model Management.

» 2000 - Age 54 - The Simpsons aired "Bart to the Future," an episode in which Trump became president of the United States.

NOTABLE QUOTABLE

"One of the key problems today is that politics is such a disgrace. Good people don't go into government."

- *President Donald J. Trump*

» 2004 - Age 58 - The Apprentice premiered. In 2004, Trump began starring in the hit NBC reality series The Apprentice, which also spawned the offshoot The Celebrity Apprentice.

THE ENTREPRENEUR'S DRAGON ENERGY

» 2004 - Age 58 - FAIL - Bankruptcy #3 - Trump Hotel and Casino Resorts

PRESS CLIPPINGS - "From mid-1995 to early 2009, Trump served as chairman of Trump Hotels and Casino Resorts (renamed Trump Entertainment Resorts in 2004), and held the CEO title for five years (mid-2000 to mid-2005). During Trump's 13 years as chairman, the casino empire lost a total of $1.1 billion, twice declared bankruptcy, and wrote down or restructured $1.8 billion in debt. Over the same period, the company paid Trump—essentially Trump paying himself—roughly $82 million by Fortune's estimates, collected from a dizzying variety of sources spelled out in the company's proxy filings, as varied as payments for use of Trump's private plane to fees paid directly Trump for access to his name and marketing expertise." - http://fortune.com/2016/03/10/trump-hotel-casinos-pay-failure

It's important to recognize the importance of the casino empire's role in Trump's vaunted mid-1990s comeback. At that time, Trump was still struggling financially from his missteps of the late '80s and early '90s.

The IPO of Trump Hotels was what finally fueled Trump's comeback, and eventually to his current highly disputed claim that he is now worth over $10 billion. That climb got its start with financing through the offering from individual and institutional investors and bond investors, which in large deals like Trump's were typically pension funds and insurance companies.

2005 - Age 58 - March 17th, 2005 - Trump began construction for the Chicago-based Trump International Hotel and Tower. The grand opening of Trump International Hotel and Tower in Chicago took place in 2009. Trump International Hotel and Tower Chicago—also called Trump Tower Chicago—is a commercial and residential skyscraper located at 401 North Wabash Avenue along the Chicago River, offering condominiums, retail space, parking facilities, and hotel services.

The tower is a 98-story structure, which reaches a height of 1,388 feet (423.2 m) including its spire, its roof topping out at 1,171 feet (357 m). It is next to the main branch of the Chicago River, with a view of the entry to Lake Michigan beyond a series of bridges over the river.

Trump announced in 2001 that the skyscraper would become the tallest building in the world, but after the September 11 attacks that same year, he scaled back the building's plans, and its design underwent several revisions.

When topped out in 2009, it became the fourth-tallest building in the US. It surpassed the city's John Hancock Center as the building with the highest residence (apartment or condo) in the world, and briefly held this title until the completion of the Burj Khalifa. The 339-room hotel opened for business with limited accommodations and services on January 30, 2008, then full accommodation and services on April 28. A restaurant on the 16th floor, Sixteen, opened in early 2008 to favorable reviews.

The building topped out in late 2008 and construction was completed in 2009. As of 2015, the hotel is among three in Chicago with an elite five-star Forbes Travel Guide rating. The restaurant is one of three five-star Forbes-rated restaurants in the city, and the spa is one of six that is at least four-star Forbes-rated in the Chicago area in 2015. Sixteen is one of five restaurants in Chicago with a Michelin Guide two-star rating in 2016.

Trump International Tower Chicago is the 2nd tallest hotel in Chicago and was named Best Large City Hotel in North America in 2010.

» 2007 - Age 60 - Trump Received star on the Hollywood Walk of Fame.

» 2008 - Age 61 - The Trump International Hotel in Las

THE ENTREPRENEUR'S DRAGON ENERGY

Vegas is opened. The Trump International Hotel Las Vegas is a 64-story luxury hotel, condominium, and timeshare located on Fashion Show Drive near Las Vegas Boulevard, just off the Las Vegas Strip in Paradise, Nevada, named for real estate developer and the 45th and current President of the United States Donald Trump.

It is located across the street from Wynn Las Vegas, behind Alon Las Vegas on 3.46 acres (14,000 m2), near the Fashion Show Mall, and features both non-residential hotel condominiums and residential condominiums. The exterior glass is infused with gold. The hotel is a member of The Leading Hotels of the World. Although Trump held a Nevada gaming license, he chose not to include a casino on the property

NOTABLE QUOTABLE

"We have no problem getting a gaming license, but we wanted to do something different here. We wanted a true luxury resort experience. It's hard to have a high-quality product when you walk into 'ding, ding, ding' and there are people walking around in Hawaiian shirts with big plastic drink mugs."

- President Donald J. Trump

» 2009 - Age 63 - FAIL - Bankruptcy #4 - Trump Entertainment Resorts

PRESS CLIPPINGS - "From mid-1995 to early 2009, Trump served as chairman of Trump Hotels and Casino Resorts (renamed Trump Entertainment Resorts in 2004), and held the CEO title for five years (mid-2000 to mid-2005). During Trump's 13 years as chairman, the casino empire lost a total of $1.1 billion, twice declared bankruptcy, and wrote down or restructured $1.8 billion in debt. Over the same period, the company paid Trump—essentially Trump paying himself—roughly $82 million by Fortune's estimates, collected from a dizzying variety of sources spelled out in the company's proxy filings, as varied as payments for use of Trump's private plane to fees paid directly Trump for access to his name and marketing expertise." - http://fortune.com/2016/03/10/trump-hotel-casinos-pay-failure

NOTABLE QUOTABLE

"One of the key problems today is that politics is such a disgrace. Good people don't go into government."

- President Donald J. Trump

> » 2012 - Age 66 - October - Trump offered Barack Obama $5 million to the charity of his choice in exchange for the president releasing his birth certificate.

> » 2017 - Age 71 - On Tuesday, November 8th, 2016, President Donald J. Trump was elected as President of the United States of America.

CHAPTER 1

DRAGON ENERGY
POWER PRINCIPLE **1**

THE DRAGON ENERGY CROSSES POLITICAL LINES

THE ENTREPRENEUR'S DRAGON ENERGY

Whether or not we agree with their politics, Kanye West and President Donald J. Trump have had undeniable success. They also have controlled a large part of the cultural conversation for the past 20 years. Although I personally believe that being successful includes being happily married to the same woman for the rest of my life and avoiding bankruptcy, our society disagrees. As you read this book, think objectively about Kanye, Trump, and the lives of other extremely successful people. Pause and sincerely seek to discover and improve your own weaknesses as we examine the lives of both of these men. Neither President Trump or Kanye West are perfect, but they also have to deal with their lives unfolding in front of the media because of their success.

ASK YOURSELF:

» In what areas do you disagree with the overall mindset, values, and worldviews of Kanye West?

_____

_____

_____

_____

» What characteristics do you find admirable in Kanye West?

_____

_____

_____

_____

» In what ways do you need to improve your work ethic to operate on the same level of passion, tenacity, and drive as Kanye West?

_____

_____

_____

_____

» In what areas do you disagree with the overall mindset, values, and worldviews of President Donald J. Trump?

_____

_____

_____

_____

» What characteristics do you find admirable in President Donald J. Trump?

_____

_____

_____

» In what ways do you need to improve your work ethic to operate on the same level of passion, tenacity, and drive as President Donald J. Trump?

_____

_____

_____

CHAPTER 2

DRAGON ENERGY POWER PRINCIPLE 2

DEVELOP THE HABIT OF DOING MORE THAN YOU ARE PAID TO DO

NOTABLE QUOTABLE

"By performing more service and better service than that for which you are paid, you not only exercise your service-rendering qualities, and thereby develop skill and ability of an extraordinary sort, but you build reputation that is valuable. If you form the habit of rendering such service you will become so adept in your work that you can command greater remuneration than those who do not perform such service."

- Napoleon Hill (The personal apprentice of Andrew Carnegie who went on to become one of the best-selling self-help authors of all time with his book, Think and Grow Rich)

ASK YOURSELF:

» On a scale of 1 to 10, with 10 being the best, how consistent are you with getting projects completed before their deadline?

_____

_____

_____

_____

» On a scale of 1 to 10, with 10 being the best, how consistent are you with delivering better results than expected from your customers or supervisor?

_____

_____

_____

» In what ways can you take your over-delivery to your current customers (or your boss) to the next level?

_____

_____

_____

» On a scale of 1 to 10, with 10 being the best, how consistent are you about getting to work on time?

_____

_____

_____

CHAPTER 3

DRAGON ENERGY
POWER PRINCIPLE 3

MASTER A SKILL THAT PAYS THE BILLS

THE ENTREPRENEUR'S DRAGON ENERGY

NOTABLE QUOTABLE

"I feel like I'm too busy writing history to read it."

- *Kanye West*

In order for us to succeed on this planet, we must become so great at something that the public cannot ignore us. In order to achieve greatness, we must be able to perform at that next level. No one wants to pay a man who is slightly above average to play professional basketball. Nobody wants to go to a concert where a mediocre musician is performing. Customers are not going to line up to pay you copious amounts of hard-earned cash to buy something that is half-assed. My friend, when we do things half-assed, our whole lives are terrible.

Now, whether you and I can relate to or appreciate Kanye West's music or not, his mastery of producing Grammy award-winning music and top 40 hits is undeniable. That is because he has devoted thousands of hours to honing his skills. Unfortunately, the vast majority of Americans are perpetually and pathetically distracted at all times. When your calendar is filled up with endless and mindless social activities, or you spend your day on Facebook wishing people that you barely know "happy birthday," it becomes very hard to focus on something long enough to ever become great.

FUN FACT:

Kanye West has won a total of 21 Grammy Awards, making him one of the most awarded artists of all time and the most Grammy-awarded artist of his generation.

President Donald Trump's net worth currently sits at $2.8 billion according to Bloomberg's 2018 estimates.

ASK YOURSELF:

» How many hours per day do you devote to watching TV?

_____

_____

_____

» How many hours per day do you devote to social media?

_____

_____

_____

» How many hours per day do you invest in talking about
political issues, religious issues, gossip, feelings, or bad things
that happened to you in the past that you cannot control?

_____

_____

_____

» How many non-productive social groups are you involved in?

_____

_____

_____

» How many dysfunctional people do you spend time with per week?

_____

_____

_____

» How many hours per week do you devote to improving
an area of your life or your business that does not directly
make you a profit?

_____

_____

_____

CHAPTER 4

DRAGON ENERGY POWER PRINCIPLE 4

REFUSE TO LOSE

THE ENTREPRENEUR'S DRAGON ENERGY

Having spent an enormous amount of time in the physical presence of people who have achieved universally recognized greatness (NBA Hall of Fame Basketball Player, David Robinson; the public relations consultant of choice for Michael Jackson, Prince, Nike, Pizza Hut, Michael Levine; the founder of the billion-dollar arts and crafts store Hobby Lobby, David Green, etc), I have noticed that they are all very competitive people. Not winning bothers them. I have also noticed people who are non-competitive are unsuccessful.

My friend, in order to dominate in this world we live in, YOU HAVE TO WANT IT and you have to want it in a DEEP-WHITE-HOT-BURNING-DESIRE-WAY, or you will lose to somebody who wants success more than you.

I have witnessed people who have been able to find this gear later in life, but it usually feels uncomfortable for someone who has never been focused on winning.

I have seen many people experience feelings of guilt because their business was doing well when they should be stepping on the gas to beat their arch rival competitor who they have been battling for years.

ASK YOURSELF:

» How competitive are you on a scale of 1 to 10, with 10 being the most competitive?

_____

_____

_____

» In what ways could you be more competitive about your work?

_____

_____

_____

» What was the last thing that you were competitive about and why?

_____

_____

_____

CHAPTER 5

DRAGON ENERGY
POWER PRINCIPLE 5

PEOPLE WHO HIT "SNOOZE" LOSE

THE ENTREPRENEUR'S DRAGON ENERGY

Virtually every time I interview a super successful person, I try to ask them about their daily routines. It's amazing how they pretty much all wake up at 5 A.M. or earlier. My friend, if you are struggling to find time to get everything done, there is a massive amount of time available between 3 A.M. and 8 A.M. One way to get your day started off right is to wake up immediately when the alarm goes off. I've noticed throughout the past 20 years as an entrepreneur that people who tend to hit the snooze button tend to lose in both business and life.

In order to win, you have to put in the time and you have to learn to rise and grind. When I drive to work at 3 A.M. in the morning, it's always amazing to me how little traffic there is. In fact, there is never any traffic when I drive to work. You can get so much more done when you wake up three hours before everybody else. I'm not sure if you are into worms or not, but the early bird does, in fact, get the worm.

ASK YOURSELF:

» What time do you wake up every day and why?

_____

_____

_____

» What time do you need to wake up every day to have the time to turn your dreams into reality?

_____

_____

_____

CHAPTER 6

DRAGON ENERGY POWER PRINCIPLE 6

BELIEVE YOU'RE THE BEST AND BACK YOUR BELIEF WITH YOUR BEST EFFORT

THE ENTREPRENEUR'S DRAGON ENERGY

As an entrepreneur, you must take massive pride in your work and you must develop the habit of not cutting corners and of consistently delivering more and better service for which you are paid to do. When you consistently overdeliver, you will begin to develop more pride in your work and a greater demand for the services and products that you provide. However, it all starts with overdelivering. If you want to stand out in the cluttered world of commerce, you simply must be committed to exceeding the expectations of every client and every boss that you have.

ASK YOURSELF:

» Are you the best in your industry and why or why not?

_____

_____

» If you are not the best in your industry, who is the best and why?

_____

_____

» What do you need to do to become the best in your industry?

_____

_____

CHAPTER 7

DRAGON ENERGY
POWER PRINCIPLE **7**

ALLOW
THE WORLD
TO WITNESS
YOUR WINNING

THE ENTREPRENEUR'S DRAGON ENERGY

It might make many people uncomfortable, but nearly all super successful people, including President Trump and Kanye West, make sure that the world knows when they win. I did not discover the power of fact-based self-promotion until I was recognized in the Tulsa World as the Young Entrepreneur of the Year by the Tulsa Chamber of Commerce. The moment that my face was featured in the newspaper people within the Tulsa market began treating me differently. I paid to have the article framed and mounted in my office, and it was amazing how clients reacted to seeing this media coverage. Although I had been DJing for many years, it was almost as if I had finally become "legit" as a result of that newspaper article and the Tulsa Chamber Award.

Since that time, I have been very intentional about making sure that we secure media coverage for our various business achievements. In addition to raising the profile of the brand and the prestige of the business overall, it also helps to improve our search engine rankings and our online reputation. Just do a quick Google search for "Tulsa Men's Haircuts" to see the online reputation for Elephant In The Room Men's Grooming Lounge, or do a search on YouTube for "Thrivetime Show Conference Reviews" and you will see the importance of showcasing your winning to the world.

ASK YOURSELF:

» When was the last time your business was featured in
local media?

_____

_____

_____

_____

» What industry awards could you apply for to earn
favorable media attention and improved brand
perception?

_____

_____

_____

_____

» How could you document your business wins better on
your website (expansion, continued growth, success of
the team, positive customer feedback)?

_____

_____

_____

_____

CHAPTER 8

DRAGON ENERGY POWER PRINCIPLE 8

LIVE AS THOUGH EVERY DAY IS YOUR LAST

THE ENTREPRENEUR'S DRAGON ENERGY

My friend, life is not a dress rehearsal - we only get one shot at this human existence (that I know of). Don't spend your days putting off doing what you know you want to do. If you want to start a new business, figure out of how much money you need to save to get started. If you want a promotion, figure out what you need to do to get promoted. Don't sit around looking depressed, walking slow, dragging your feet and yawning all of the time. People who bring energy and positivity to their jobs win because of it. People who are aimlessly drifting through life take bottom paying jobs because they are bottom feeders who bring the least amount of effort to their work.

Today, I went to the gas station and met a sad loser, who I hope will learn this lesson soon. This young man works at a gas station en route to my office, and I witnessed him respond to a customer's question in a way that shows he isn't going anywhere with his life. He wants everybody to know about it so that he can repel any opportunities that he might have normally had.

The customer said, "Hello, how are you?"

The clerk replied, "Well it's just another day," followed by a sigh of disgust.

My friends, I have seen this clerk in action enough to know that he specializes in bringing negativity, sarcasm, and low energy to all situations, which is why he is not promotable.

He obviously doesn't view this job as a means to any ends. He leaves his station to go out and vape in front of the gas station at any chance he gets, and when he's not doing that, he's using his personal smartphone to call somebody who is not the customer standing right in front of him.

ASK YOURSELF:

» On a scale of 1 to 10, how intentional are you about seizing each and every day?

_____

_____

_____

_____

» On a scale of 1 to 10, how good are you at being a self-starter and why?

_____

_____

_____

_____

» If you are drifting aimlessly through life right now, what do you need to do to stop drifting (an accountability partner, a challenge, a coach, a support group, a kick in the pants, a police-grade taser, etc)?

_____

_____

_____

_____

CHAPTER 9

DRAGON ENERGY
POWER PRINCIPLE **9**

SET HUGE, BEAUTIFUL GOALS

THE ENTREPRENEUR'S DRAGON ENERGY

Whether we agree with it or not, nobody wants to work with or for somebody who has small goals. Nobody wants to celebrate the lives of people who don't achieve anything.

What are your goals for the next year in the following six categories?

» Faith

_____

_____

_____

_____

» Family

_____

_____

_____

_____

» Finances

_____

_____

_____

_____

» Fitness

_____

_____

_____

_____

» Friendship

_____

_____

_____

_____

» Fun

_____

_____

_____

_____

CHAPTER 10

DRAGON ENERGY
POWER PRINCIPLE **10**

TURN THEIR HATE INTO YOUR FUEL

THE ENTREPRENEUR'S DRAGON ENERGY

I discovered haters for the first time when my first business DJConnection. com began to take off. I would get voicemails from competitors, who I had never met, discouraging me and telling me that our service was crap. It was unbelievable that adult men in their 30s were taking time out of their schedules to leave negative messages on my voicemail. I was 21 and beginning to land huge business accounts with the likes of Bama Companies, Boeing Airlines, QuikTrip, Caterpillar, etc, which meant that they were losing those large corporate entertainment accounts. They hated me for winning and for beating them. It took me almost a year to get to a place where I actually became thankful for the hate of the competition and the naysayers. Today, believe it or not, I'm actually very grateful for the haters because they always inspire me to dominate even more.

ASK YOURSELF:

» Who are your current haters?

_____

_____

_____

» On a scale of 1 to 10, with 10 being the best, how well are you doing with the negative emotions caused by haters and why?

_____

_____

_____

From time to time, I release what I call a "Lyrical Miracle" on the Thrivetime Show. These are essentially rap songs with a deep thoughts that I am trying to communicate to a large audience. One of these songs is called "There Is No Justice, There Is Just Us." As it relates to dealing with haters, I think that you will find the lyrics of this song to be powerful and accurate.

"There is No Justice, There Is Just Us"

VERSE 1

There is no justice, there is just us
Like Matthew 5:10 straight promised us
I couldn't count all the traitors with an abacus
That gossip and betray like the name Judas
Coat tail riding maggots they leach and fuss
With their slack hands tryin' to turn my shine to rust
But it's time for them to go, start their bus
Cuz hence forth in only GOD above I trust
As I got rich slow they complained and fussed
That their fame hadn't happened with words they cut
But my heart no longer bleeds, it's stone enough
To withstand backstabbing and their endless cuts
I'm a wife man, straight monogamous
Let their disease and shame be the judge
I've been on Earth too long and seen to much
To ever let people in again it's too dangerous
No trojan horses behind my walls and such
Like it's Hammer time, they can longer touch
It's like Shimmy Shimmy Yah, Shimmy Sham, Shimmy Yay
Fake friends and family get the hell out of my way

THE ENTREPRENEUR'S DRAGON ENERGY

VERSE 2

Like an excuse me, BEEP here comes the bus
This is my year to run over those that I cannot trust
And although I'm calm on the service, like a business duck
I've been paddling below the water, and now what's up
Like a squirrel in the spring I've been saving up nuts

And their Winter is coming, and there
could be famine and such
There will be famine in land, and life could get tough
For all those names on my list who have minimum bucks
We live an F6 Life, but there is a secret F, hush
And like Limbaugh, they'll be schooled in a Rush

You see I built the systems and I own all the stuff
And my love bank is empty and I don't give a what?
I thought he was a Christian man and all that stuff?
Who reads 1st Samuel 15:3 for good luck
You it's time for me to take away Tiny Tim's crutch

And when their dominos fall, I'll be just warming up.

CHAPTER 11

DRAGON ENERGY POWER PRINCIPLE 11

DEVELOP AN ACTION BIAS

THE ENTREPRENEUR'S DRAGON ENERGY

The average person will allow their emotions to block their motions. However, whenever you spend time with SUPER SUCCESSFUL people, you will notice that they are always on the go and have a tremendous bias for action. When you are around people who have never achieved success as an entrepreneur, you will notice that they have a bias towards passivity and ask endless doubt-filled questions until all momentum and energy is gone and then they will ask more questions like:

- » Where are they all going to sit?

- » What if it doesn't work?

- » Is it legal?

- » Is it ethical?

- » What matters more, family or work?

- » I think we should run it by a committee.

- » Has it ever been done before?

- » Maybe we should try to get a government grant for that?

NOTABLE QUOTABLE

"Do not spend too much time planning or trying to anticipate and solve problems before they happen. That is just another kind of excuse for procrastination. Until you start, you won't know where the problems will occur. You won't have the experience to solve them. Instead, get into action, and solve the problems as they arise."

- President Donald J. Trump

Enormously successful people are always "on the go" and "moving," while the "ponderers" and "intenders" never get anything done. Those people tend to spend their lives endlessly questioning the following aspects of every decision over and over until they reach the point of paralysis by analysis:

- » Does everybody approve of this idea?
- » Is this the best possible idea?
- » Are we 100% sure this idea will work?
- » Who do we know that has already done this idea before?
- » What if this idea doesn't work?

NOTABLE QUOTABLE

"Success seems to be connected with action. Successful people keep moving. They make mistakes, but they don't quit."

- Conrad Hilton (The action-focused founder of the Hilton Hotel chain)

THE ENTREPRENEUR'S DRAGON ENERGY

ASK YOURSELF:

» In what areas of your business are you struggling with
paralysis by analysis?

_____

_____

_____

» Who in your business has a bias for procrastination
instead of action?

_____

_____

_____

» On a scale of 1 to 10 with 10 being the highest, how
would you rate your bias for action?

_____

_____

_____

» On a scale of 1 to 10 with 10 being the best, how would
you rate your team's bias for action?

_____

_____

_____

» Who are spending time with that is killing your
momentum?

_____

_____

_____

» Who in your life has an action and the entrepreneurial mindset that you wish to develop?

_____

_____

CHAPTER 12

DRAGON ENERGY POWER PRINCIPLE 12

TURN TRAGEDY INTO TRIUMPH

THE ENTREPRENEUR'S DRAGON ENERGY

We all experience tough times, tragedy, and betrayal to some extent, but very successful people always seem to find a way to turn their frustration into motivation. My friend, as you begin to grow an organization, you will discover that with more money comes more responsibility, more interactions with more people. So, even if you surround yourself with a high-character group of employees and teammates, you are still going to experience a minimum of twice the amount of issues and tragedies as the average person just because you know more people.

ASK YOURSELF:

» On a scale of 1 to 10, with 10 being the highest, how highly would you rate your ability to turn tragedy into triumph and why?

_____

_____

_____

_____

» What is an area in your life that you are lamenting and marinating on instead of letting it go and moving on?

_____

_____

_____

_____

» What is an area of bitterness in your life that you have successfully been able to turn into betterness and positive motivation?

_____

_____

_____

CHAPTER 13

DRAGON ENERGY
POWER PRINCIPLE **13**

BECOME A PASSIONATE SELF-PROMOTER

THE ENTREPRENEUR'S DRAGON ENERGY

Like it or not, the squeaky wheel gets the oil. I've witnessed countless of low-skilled self-promoters in charge of big organizations simply because they are always the first one to speak up and let people know that they are hungry for the opportunity, the job, or the deal. In my own career, I have landed huge and critical accounts for my businesses simply because I decided to become my own biggest fan around the age of 16. Trust me, nothing is worse than knowing that you are perpetually overqualified and overlooked because you are consciously making an effort to not become a self-promoter.

» What deals and opportunities have you missed out on because you simply refused to promote yourself?

» If you don't believe in self-promotion, are you willing to hire a publicist or a hype-man to promote you?

» If you are against self-promotion of any kind where do you draw the line?

**NOTE: I am 100% certain that I would not be married to my wife Vanessa if I was not able to shamelessly promote myself and the future that I could give her. The tricky part was being able to live up to my own hype after we got married.

CHAPTER 14

DRAGON ENERGY
POWER PRINCIPLE **14**

BRING THE DRAGON ENERGY 100% OF THE TIME YOU ARE WORKING

THE ENTREPRENEUR'S DRAGON ENERGY

My partner, Doctor Robert Zoellner, is always talking about this concept he calls, "showtime." Showtime is essentially about choosing to be positive, "on," and in character 100% of the time when you are in front of prospective clients, current clients, prospective employees, and current employees. I sincerely believe in the power of showtime, which is why I prefer to spend the vast majority of my weekends and nights alone. I enjoy being "off" and wearing a hoodie sweatshirt while watching a Patriots Game, burning pinon wood while not talking to anyone for five consecutive hours. People might act like they care, but employees, customers, partners, and teammates don't want to hear about your personal issues, some weird rash you have, or your marital problems. Be "on," 100% of the time when you are in front of people and you will attract more success.

ASK YOURSELF:

» What could you do to bring your A-Game to the workplace more often?

_____

_____

_____

_____

CHAPTER 15

DRAGON ENERGY POWER PRINCIPLE **15**

BECOME AN OUTSPOKEN ENEMY OF AVERAGE

THE ENTREPRENEUR'S DRAGON ENERGY

Because I am filled with "Dragon Energy," I have noticed that as you rise to the top, the vast majority of people will try to pull you down with nonsensical, feelings-based discussions. They will encourage you to "remember where you came from" and not to "leave people behind." For example, I worked with a client years ago who was very physically fit, but used to be very out of shape in the past. He went from being very unhealthy to being the king of fitness in his own mind, but his heavy-set partying friends didn't know what to do with him. They really didn't like him because he wouldn't go out to the bars or go out to eat at Hooters with them anymore. These heavy-set partiers could have changed their diets and started working out at the gym with him, but they chose not to and began to resent and mock him for being in such great shape.

My friend, you must beware of people who will try to bring you down because they are threatened by your success. You also must be aware that no product is so good that it will sell itself. You must become the 100% sold-out hype man for your own products and services because nobody else will be. You must become so fired up and filled up with conviction that your product or service is the best that your entire team, your customers, and the media recognizes that you are not kidding when you claim that your product is the best.

with negative thinking and negative-acting people.
As you grow, your associates will change. Some of
your friends will not want you to go on. They will want
you to stay where they are. Friends that don't help
you climb will want you to crawl. Your friends will
stretch your vision or choke your dream. Those that
don't increase you will eventually decrease you."

- Colin Powell

NOTABLE QUOTABLE

"Consider this: Never receive counsel from unproductive
people. Never discuss your problems with someone
incapable of contributing to the solution, because those
who never succeed themselves are always first to tell
you how. Not everyone has a right to speak into your
life. You are certain to get the worst of the bargain
when you exchange ideas with the wrong person.
Don't follow anyone who's not going anywhere."

- Colin Powell

ASK YOURSELF:

» In what ways are you tolerating mediocrity around you in
the workplace?

_____

_____

_____

_____

» In what ways are you tolerating mediocrity in your
home?

_____

_____

_____

_____

» In what ways are you tolerating mediocrity in your marriage or relationship?

_____

_____

_____

» In what ways are you tolerating mediocrity in your fitness?

_____

_____

_____

_____

» In what ways are you tolerating mediocrity in your friendships?

_____

_____

_____

_____

» In what ways are you tolerating mediocrity in your finances?

_____

_____

_____

_____

» In what ways are you tolerating mediocrity in your habits?

_____

_____

_____

CHAPTER 16

DRAGON ENERGY POWER PRINCIPLE 16

JUDGE PEOPLE BASED ON WHAT THEY DO

THE ENTREPRENEUR'S DRAGON ENERGY

NOTABLE QUOTABLE

"I judge people based on their capability, honesty, and merit."

- President Donald J. Trump

We live on a planet where people run around saying "only God can judge me." It's socially acceptable to get nifty tattoos that state "Only God Can Judge Me," but that's not how life works. People are constantly judging each other based on the words we use, the people we associate with, the clothes we wear, and the results that we deliver. In fact, over time—whether it's fair or not—the people who know you best will begin to formulate a long-term judgment about you, and that's called a "reputation."

NOTABLE QUOTABLE

"As I grow older, I pay less attention to what men say. I just watch what they do."

- Andrew Carnegie (The world's wealthiest man during his lifetime was forced to work at just the age of 13 to support his struggling immigrant family. Carnegie's first job in 1848 was as a bobbin boy, changing spools of thread in a cotton mill 12 hours a day, six days a week in a Pittsburgh cotton factory. His starting wage was $1.20 per week—$34 by 2017 inflation)

When you have a burning desire to achieve success at the next level, the bogus limitations and obligations imposed on you by the people around you will simply become irrelevant. As an example, in 1938, President Franklin Delano Roosevelt created what is now known as the "40 Hour Work Week."

However, up until that time in world history, people always had to work until the job was done. In fact, the first book of the Bible (Genesis) establishes the pattern of working for six consecutive days and then resting on the seventh day. The Bible goes on to teach this principle in Exodus 16:5 where it reads, "On the sixth day they are to prepare what they bring in, and that is to be twice as much as they gather on the other days." In Exodus 20:11, we find the text that reads, "For in six days the Lord made the heavens and the earth and all that is in them, but he rested on the seventh day." In Exodus 16:22, readers can also find the passage that reads, "On the sixth day, they gathered twice as much for each person, and the leaders of the community came and reported this to Moses."

What if the Pilgrims believed in the 40 hour work week? Would they have even survived? What if legendary NFL coach Bill Belichick, believed in the 40-hour work week? Could he have achieved success at the level he has today? If you are not willing to invest 60 to 80 hours per week to turn your dreams into reality, then you might as well deposit them in the closest toilet you can find.

NOTABLE QUOTABLE

"In the end, you're measured not by how much you undertake, but by what you finally accomplish."

- President Donald J. Trump

I know that this idea blows the minds of many people, but in a capitalistic society you are judged by what you actually do and not just based upon what you intend to do. Although many churches, schools, local coffee shops, and support groups will say that you are "amazing" and "fabulous" just as a result of being born, I am here to tell you that nobody gives a crap about your "potential" and your "value as a human being."

THE ENTREPRENEUR'S DRAGON ENERGY

Our incredible God above may love you unconditionally and may treat you as though you are a member of his royal kingdom, but the people at the store don't accept your "divine royalty" as a form of payment. In fact, you can't buy anything with your "awesomeness." Thus, if you ever want to exchange currency for the goods and services that you want on this planet, you are going to have to actually generate results.

Even though it would be easier for me to tell you that results don't matter, they do. In fact, results are what really matter on this planet. If you don't believe that, then you are probably being supported by the tax dollars of somebody who produces results, or by a family member who produced results so that you can use their money to sustain yourself. In our offices, I wrote the following text just above our urinals:

"Quick Note to Employees:
1. I see you texting, Instagramming, etc.
2. I do record your keystrokes
3. I do judge you based upon what you do."

— CLAY CLARK 2017

ASK YOURSELF:

How effective have you been as a human thus far when it comes to achieving results?

_____

_____

_____

_____

Financially speaking, how happy are you with your results up to this point in your life?

_____

_____

If you are going to be judged in the game of business based on how well you do, how highly would you be ranked thus far with 1 being the highest and 10 being the lowest, and why?

_____

_____

_____

_____

On a scale of 1 to 10, with 10 being the highest, how would the people you work with rate your work ethic and why?

_____

_____

_____

_____

If Steve Jobs, Kanye West, President Trump, Tom Brady, Oprah, and Michael Jordan have a level 10 work ethic, how highly would you rank your own work ethic and why?

_____

_____

_____

_____

Name one successful entrepreneur who worked less than six days per week en route to starting their successful and sustainable business?

_____

_____

_____

_____

CHAPTER 17

DRAGON ENERGY POWER PRINCIPLE 17

BE WILLING TO CONSISTENTLY DO WHATEVER IT TAKES TO WIN (AS LONG AS IT'S NOT ILLEGAL OR SINFUL)

THE ENTREPRENEUR'S DRAGON ENERGY

Upon further review, it takes a lot of praying, wishing, and hoping to make up for a lack of doing. In fact, starting a business is always tough, which is why I do not recommend that the vast majority of people start their own businesses. It will only bring heartache to the families of the people involved in the business when the owner is not willing to be "all in" and do "whatever it takes."

ASK YOURSELF:

» On a scale of 1 to 10, with 10 being the best, how would you rank your ability to consistently do whatever it takes to make your business successful and why?

_____

_____

_____

_____

» What are the clear boundaries that you have for what you are willing to do, and not do, to achieve success?

_____

_____

_____

_____

CHAPTER 18

DRAGON ENERGY POWER PRINCIPLE 18

CAN'T KNOCK THE HUSTLE

THE ENTREPRENEUR'S DRAGON ENERGY

NOTABLE QUOTABLE

"But for me to have the opportunity to stand in front of a bunch of executives and present myself, I had to hustle in my own way. I can't tell you how frustrating it was that they didn't get that. No joke - I'd leave meetings crying all the time."

- Kanye West

All super successful people rise and grind, and for most of them that means waking up before 6 A.M. and grinding until the work is done. Every super successful person I've met has always worked six to seven days per week during the early stages of their business to ensure its success. My friend, I struggle being in the physical presence of lazy people.

I cannot understand them, and I honestly do not want to understand their constant complaining about their current boss, their past boss, their "tough 40 hours spent on their feet" (40 hours is approximately ½ of the time required for any startup entrepreneur to work every week until the business is sustainably successful and off of life support), their boredom with their careers, or their constant belief that they are being overlooked by leadership for the tremendous accomplishments that they bring to the workplace each week in exchange for a paycheck.

NOTABLE QUOTABLE

"Everything negative - pressure, challenges - is all an opportunity for me to rise.These young guys are playing checkers. I'm out there playing chess.I don't want to be the next Michael Jordan, I only want to be Kobe Bryant"

- Kobe Bryant (Former Professional NBA Player for the Los Angeles Lakers for 20 years)

People who are filled with "Dragon Energy" are very aware of the Law of Cause and Effect. They understand that hard work creates results. They understand that cold calls produce appointments. They understand that no sick days creates the habit of consistency. They understand that accountability creates traction. They understand that firing idiots creates a positive work environment. And they understand that whoever adds the most relevant original HTML content to their website gets to be awarded with the top spot in the Google search engine results. To succeed, you must embrace, know, and learn to benefit from the Law of Cause and Effect.

ASK YOURSELF:

» In what areas have you been passively sitting back and waiting for success to come your way?

_____

_____

_____

_____

» In what ways have you been hoping for life to change without taking any action to turn your current reality into your ideal reality?

_____

_____

_____

_____

» In what ways have you been acting as though the Law of Cause and Effect is not relevant to you?

_____

_____

_____

_____

CHAPTER 19

DRAGON ENERGY
POWER PRINCIPLE **19**

EXCHANGE AN EYE FOR AN ENTIRE BODY

THE ENTREPRENEUR'S DRAGON ENERGY

Successful people guard their reputation with their life and they will do whatever they have to do to protect it. In fact, countless times throughout my own life, I have had to fight for my reputation. Years ago, while I was building DJConnection.com, one of our key people left the company to start his own company (as dozens of people did). However, when this particular individual left the company, he told people that he had to leave the company for "ethical reasons". This is the same employee who had to be fired for routinely showing up to work late, drunk, or in other states of mental impairment. In spite of all of that, his story sounded good to many of the people who did not know me as the emotionally, mentally, and financially stable father of five kids that I am.

Thus, when I began to hear of the rumors spreading throughout the wedding industry, I had to schedule time to meet with dozens of wedding vendors to set the story straight and to encourage them to invest the time needed to look up this person's publicly available criminal record. You see my friend, that is the great thing about how Google now indexes the internet. When somebody commits a sex crime, their mugshot and their crime now pulls up along with their name. During this time of reputation management, many of my peers within the wedding industry who do not possess the "Dragon Energy" told me that I was being harsh, but I would not stop sharing the "Good News" that this former employee was "Bad News." Eventually, he wasn't able to land a gig within the city of Tulsa, and I could have stopped, but I chose not to.

I continued sharing the "truth" with every wedding vendor I could until this man ultimately had to leave town—but not before he was left by his wife for having an extra-marital affair. My friend, in the world of business, you must protect your name and reputation at all costs. You must make sure that you do not allow your name to be slandered by morally-depraved underperformers who have nothing to lose -- because they will try.

ASK YOURSELF:

» How have you let competitors passively destroy your reputation?

_____

_____

_____

_____

» In your business career, when have you sat back and let people destroy your business' name withoutputting up a fight?

_____

_____

_____

_____

» What is an area of your life that is worth fighting for?

_____

_____

_____

_____

CHAPTER 20

DRAGON ENERGY
POWER PRINCIPLE 20

BURN BRIDGES TO CREATE DISTANCE

THE ENTREPRENEUR'S DRAGON ENERGY

Being aware that the people around you are either bringing you up or pulling you down is a powerful concept once you finally get it, accept it, and act upon it. I used to have stupid meetings in my office filled with discussions about feelings. The mentally and emotionally lazy people would consistently suggest half-baked and non-actionable ideas mixed with a never-ending supply of excuses. I used to have an email inbox filled with long emails sent by people with short attention spans, and a calendar filled with obligations and special occasions attended by people unable to engage in intelligent conversations. Now, all of that is gone. Why? Because I burned bridges to create separation, and I dramatically upgraded my social circle to upgrade my quality of life. Were there some rough conversations? Yes. Are there some people that I will never talk to again? Yes. And I could not be happier.

ASK YOURSELF:

» Are you an asset or a liability to the people that know you?

_____

_____

_____

» Do you typically bring the energy in the room up or down when you enter it, and why?

_____

_____

_____

» Who are the people in your life pulling you down with their excuses, their drama, and their negativity?

_____

_____

_____

_____

» Who are the people in your life that you need to be spending more time with?

_____

_____

_____

_____

CHAPTER 21

DRAGON ENERGY POWER PRINCIPLE 21

PRESIDENTIAL ASPIRATIONS (AIM FOR THE HIGHEST POSSIBLE POSITION)

THE ENTREPRENEUR'S DRAGON ENERGY

Whether you want to be the president of the United States or the best dad in American history, all successful people set MASSIVE goals that no one else thinks are possible. Most people aim low so that they won't run the risk of being rejected. However, all successful people that I have met shoot for the stars so even when they miss, they hit the moon.

ASK YOURSELF:

» What are a few goals that you have for your family that you've been putting off because they are so big that they scare you?

_____

_____

_____

» What are a few financial and career goals that you have buried deep down inside of you that are so big that they scare you?

_____

_____

_____

CHAPTER 22

DRAGON ENERGY
POWER PRINCIPLE 22

STOP BEING POLITICALLY CORRECT AND GET DOWN TO BUSINESS

THE ENTREPRENEUR'S DRAGON ENERGY

Once you've reached the top you no longer have to worry about playing the political correctness game. Successful people are so focused on achieving their goals and living up to their own moral standards, that they are not typically concerned about what anyone else thinks. Thus, when they are asked direct questions, they tend to give direct answers. Many people find to be harsh in our modern, easily-offended culture of political correctness. On a cautionary note, know that if you ask a super successful person a direct question you will more than likely get a direct answer.

But in life, there is right and there is wrong; there is up and there is down; there is fit and there is fat; there is tall and there is short; there is good food and there is bad food. People with "Dragon Energy" tend to view the world in terms of black and white.

ASK YOURSELF:

> » In what ways has your refusal to take a hard stance
> on something hurt your career and your life?

_____

_____

_____

> » In what ways has being too direct with people—before you
> have the leverage to do so—hurt your career and your life?

_____

_____

_____

CHAPTER 23

DRAGON ENERGY
POWER PRINCIPLE 23

OPERATE ON AN ENTIRELY DIFFERENT LEVEL

THE ENTREPRENEUR'S DRAGON ENERGY

NOTABLE QUOTABLE

"All of us know people who are ambitious but couldn't find their way out of a burning building. However, for super successful people their level of ambition and obsession is something deeper, more primal, more intense than ambition. It is a burning, maniacal rage as if their life depended on it. That, my dear valued friend, is what is at the core, the DNA of the super successful people."

- Michael Levine

Typically, if you ask 1,000 people what their goals are for the future, they will tell you that they want to become successful. When you ask them specifically what that means for them and when they want to achieve it, that's when the conversation tends to fall apart. My friend, goals are simply dreams with deadlines. Until you put a deadline on the achievement of your goals, you are just a drifter with better packaging. If you want to become super successful, you must set specific goals with specific deadlines, and you must operate with the burning, maniacal sense of urgency needed to turn those dreams into reality. This world owes you nothing, and what the world gives you for free typically isn't worth much.

NOTABLE QUOTABLE

"No one cares about your business and your success as much or more than you."

- Doctor Robert Zoellner

ASK YOURSELF:

» In what ways can you increase your intensity about achieving your goals?

_____

_____

_____

» In what ways can you improve the specificity of your goals and your plans to achieve them?

_____

_____

_____

CHAPTER 24

DRAGON ENERGY
POWER PRINCIPLE **24**

SET YOUR OWN STANDARDS

THE ENTREPRENEUR'S DRAGON ENERGY

NOTABLE QUOTABLE

"I refuse to accept other people's ideas of happiness for me. As if there's a 'one size fits all' standard for happiness."

- Kanye West

You must find a way to inspire yourself on a daily basis and to set your own standards for your life because if you wait for somebody else to come along to inspire you, you will lose. I am writing this book in my "Man Cave," which I love. It is located on over 15 acres of land behind a wall. In this room, there are well over 100 quotes and phrases that I find to be inspirational. I ripped out the ceiling tiles so that all of the duct work is visible. I then painted the ceiling black and installed over 20 Edison bulbs because I like the look. The walls are additionally decorated with New England Patriots swag, American Flags, photos of entrepreneurial tycoons, elephants, the letter "Z," and tons of audio equipment because this is what makes me happy. Having been around so many super successful people, I have found that they all tend to create the atmosphere that they want as opposed to just accepting their home as is.

Very successful people tend to customize and modify everything in their physical space to match their goals and desires, and then that extends to nearly every area of their life. When I was 12, I moved to Minnesota and was hell bent on leaving as soon as I graduated. When I finished college, I was 100% focused on not spending time with nearly all of the people I had met in college because they were not essential to the achievement of my goals. We did not have anything in common other than the geographic location that we once shared.

You must understand that inspiration is the reward, inaction really is your giant, and that action is your sword. If you are not happy with your faith, your family, your friendships, your finances, your fitness, or your fun, I would encourage you to change them.

NOTABLE QUOTABLE

"All successful people men and women are big dreamers. They imagine what their future could be, ideal in every respect, and then they work every day toward their distant vision, that goal or purpose."

- Brian Tracy (Best-selling author and internationally renowned sales trainer and business speaker)

ASK YOURSELF:

» In what areas of your life are you discontent?

_____

_____

_____

» In what ways could you enhance your schedule to make it more favorable?

_____

_____

_____

» In what ways could you upgrade your social circle to spend more time with achievers and those who aspire to achieve, and less time with the complainers, whiners, and negative people on this planet in your proximity?

_____

_____

_____

CHAPTER 25

DRAGON ENERGY
POWER PRINCIPLE 25

REFUSE TO HIRE, SPEND TIME WITH, AND ASSOCIATE WITH LOW ENERGY PEOPLE

THE ENTREPRENEUR'S DRAGON ENERGY

Being around low energy people actually makes me very uncomfortable. I
know their mindset is wrong and it has the power to infect a whole room
of people. For the same reason that I would never invite members of the
Nazi Party over for dinner, I would avoid low energy people like the plague.

ASK YOURSELF:

» Who in your life is sucking your soul with their
   contagious low energy?

_____

_____

_____

» How would you rate your own personal energy? Are you
   a low energy human who brings the room down, or do
   you light up the room when you enter it?

_____

_____

_____

CHAPTER 26

DRAGON ENERGY POWER PRINCIPLE 26

DESTROY YOUR ENEMIES COMPLETELY

THE ENTREPRENEUR'S DRAGON ENERGY

Talking about this idea really freaks people out who choose not to operate with "Dragon Energy" because they believe that everybody deserves a second chance, a third chance, or endless chances. Most people will continue to allow the same toxic family members into their life year after year, and the same dramatic people to ruin every day at the office. Throughout my career as a speaker, consultant and coach, I've met hundreds of business owners who have been screwed over by a person they have repeatedly welomed back into their lives or their business.

I've seen business people dealing with nagging negativity in their offices for decades. If you are unwilling to kick negative individuals out of your life and business, then you need to accept that your life will always be terrible and quit complaining about it.

Personally, I view people as either healthy, vegetable-producing plants, or weeds in my garden that are trying to choke out and kill the growth

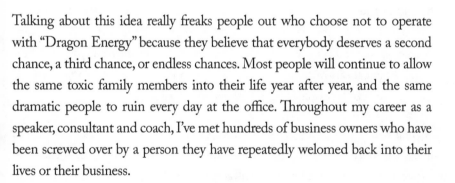

of any healthy, vegetable-producing plants. When I see a weed I pull it. When I see a healthy plant I nurture it. People with "Dragon Energy," view employees, acquaintances and all humans as being for them or against them.

NOTABLE QUOTABLE

"Anybody who hits me, we're gonna hit 10 times harder."

- President Donald J. Trump

As a caveat to this principle, I must clarify that all successful people view their business as their golden goose, and anybody that attacks their golden goose is an enemy. Thus, they will do whatever that needs to be done legally to put a stop to it. Super successful people view their business as their fresh water supply. Imagine for a second that you lived in the desert and the only fresh water for miles was found within your oasis. If you heard that people were plotting to poison your water supply, what would you do? Most people would not just sit back passively and watch their only source of fresh water get destroyed without putting up a fight. Super successful people view any attack on their business with this sense of urgency. We are all very aware of the legal ramifications of punching people, which is why we tend to not actually physically assault people ... although we often want to.

When you have a cancerous growth in your body, in your business, or in your life, it's important that you cut it out as soon as it makes sense to do so, and this especially true when working with family. It took me way too long to accept these harsh realities of life, but once I did, my life improved dramatically.

As a little encouragement, I would suggest you read 1 Samuel 15 verses 1 through 10. You might want to start with chapter 14 and go through 16 to get the true context of the situation.

THE ENTREPRENEUR'S DRAGON ENERGY

NOTABLE QUOTABLE

Samuel said to Saul, "I am the one the Lord sent to anoint you king over his people Israel; so listen now to the message from the Lord. This is what the Lord Almighty says: 'I will punish the Amalekites for what they did to Israel when they waylaid them as they came up from Egypt. Now go, attack the Amalekites and totally destroy all that belongs to them. Do not spare them; put to death men and women, children and infants, cattle and sheep, camels and donkeys.'" So Saul summoned the men and mustered them at Telaim—two hundred thousand foot soldiers and ten thousand from Judah. Saul went to the city of Amalek and set an ambush in the ravine. Then he said to the Kenites, "Go away, leave the Amalekites so that I do not destroy you along with them; for you showed kindness to all the Israelites when they came up out of Egypt." So the Kenites moved away from the Amalekites.

Then Saul attacked the Amalekites all the way from Havilah to Shur, near the eastern border of Egypt. He took Agag king of the Amalekites alive, and all his people he totally destroyed with the sword. But Saul and the army spared Agag and the best of the sheep and cattle, the fat calves and lambs—everything that was good. These they were unwilling to destroy completely, but everything that was despised and weak they totally destroyed. Then the word of the Lord came to Samuel: "I regret that I have made Saul king, because he has turned away from me and has not carried out my instructions." Samuel was angry, and he cried out to the Lord all that night."

- 1 Samuel 15:1–10

NOTABLE QUOTABLE

"My motto is: Always get even. When somebody screws you, screw them back in spades."

- President Donald J. Trump

ASK YOURSELF:

» Always ask, "Are they for me or against me?"

_____

_____

_____

» What friends of your enemies do you need to remove from your life.

_____

_____

_____

» In what ways are you allowing your competitors attack your business?

_____

_____

_____

» In what ways are you allowing passive-aggressive employees to harm your reputation?

_____

_____

_____

» In what ways are you allowing people within your life to negatively impact your quality of life?

_____

_____

_____

» Who in your life is a definite enemy?

_____

_____

_____

CHAPTER 27

DRAGON ENERGY POWER PRINCIPLE 27

HEADLINE HUNT

THE ENTREPRENEUR'S DRAGON ENERGY

NOTABLE QUOTABLE

"One thing I've learned about the press is that they're always hungry for a good story, and the more sensational the better. It's in the nature of the job, and I understand that. The point is that if you are a little different, or a little outrageous, or if you do things that are bold or controversial, the press is going to write about you."

- President Donald J. Trump

Both Kanye West and President Donald Trump have mastered the skill of sustaining a presence in the media at nearly all times, and it is truly amazing. Both Kanye and Trump seem to have read Michael Levine's public relations training masterpiece, *Guerilla P.R. 2.0 - Wage an Effective Publicity Campaign Without Going Broke.* If you are reading this and you have no idea how to get your business to be consistently featured in the local, regional, and national media conversation I would highly recommend that you read Michael's book. However, as a matter of principle, I would also encourage you to take notes the next time President Trump or Kanye speak and notice how they intentionally use figures of speech, controversial statements, scandal, shock and awe, hyperbole, and apophasis to create the media attention they seek.

NOTABLE QUOTABLE

"The final key to the way I promote is bravado. I play to people's fantasies. People may not always think big themselves, but they can get very excited by those who do. That is why a little hyperbole never hurts. People want to believe that something is the biggest, the greatest, and the most spectacular."

- President Donald J. Trump

As a Judeo-Christian, I certainly do not agree with all of President Trump's or Kanye West's publicity stunts or the way they constantly headline hunt, but I cannot argue with their results.

NOTABLE QUOTABLE

"Why would Kim Jong-un insult me by calling me 'old' when I would NEVER call him 'short and fat.' Oh well, I try so hard to be his friend and maybe someday that will happen."

- President Donald J. Trump

Super successful people use language differently—and much more confidently—than the average person. Successful people tend to talk with a declarative tone. Average people always sound like they are finishing their sentences with a question mark? You can sense the sincerely crippling doubt found in their communication style. To help demonstrate the difference between how successful people communicate and how unsuccessful people communicate, I have made the following examples for your educational benefit.

SUPER SUCCESSFUL PEOPLE WOULD SAY:

» "That movie is the best movie I've ever seen. The plot, the soundtrack, and the actors were incredible."

» "I am 100% certain that I will be at your birthday party. I've committed to it, and it's on my calendar."

UNSUCCESSFUL PEOPLE WOULD SAY:

» "The movie was okay, I guess. It sort of depends on what kind of movies you like, if that makes sense?"

» "I will try to make it to your birthday party. I'm pretty sure I'll be able to be there. What time was it again?"

THE ENTREPRENEUR'S DRAGON ENERGY

ASK YOURSELF:

» What local event could you organize to get your company the media attention you seek?

_____

_____

_____

» In what industry could you promote yourself as an expert?

_____

_____

_____

» Which celebrity could you team up with to generate media features for your company?

_____

_____

_____

» How could you change the exterior of your business to generate a buzz and become the talk of the town?

_____

_____

_____

» How could you change or improve your products or services to make them stand out in a more pronounced way?

_____

_____

_____

CHAPTER 28

DRAGON ENERGY POWER PRINCIPLE 28

INSIST THAT YOU PERSIST

THE ENTREPRENEUR'S DRAGON ENERGY

NOTABLE QUOTABLE

"For me, giving up is harder than trying."

- *Kanye West*

Do not blame God, the economy, your parents, or anything for your lack of success; just get up and keep going. If you are going through hell, that is a bad place to stop. When you refuse to blame your circumstances and you begin to accept responsibility for where you are at in life - you have power.

ASK YOURSELF:

» Who have you been blaming for your struggles?

_____

_____

_____

» In what ways have you refused to quit?

_____

_____

_____

» In what ways have you quit?

_____

_____

_____

CHAPTER 29

DRAGON ENERGY POWER PRINCIPLE 29

GET BETTER, NOT BITTER

THE ENTREPRENEUR'S DRAGON ENERGY

No one who has achieved success believes they are exceptional merely as a result of being born; they believe that their exceptional work ethic is what separates them from every one else. We live in a world where people choose to remain victims for their entire lives, so you must be careful to be intentional about turning all bitterness into betterness.

ASK YOURSELF:

» Who has hurt you the most during your life?

_____

_____

_____

» When are you going to let those hurts and betrayals go?

_____

_____

_____

CHAPTER 30

DRAGON ENERGY POWER PRINCIPLE **30**

CHERISH YOUR DREAMS AS IF THEY ARE THE CHILDREN OF YOUR SOUL

THE ENTREPRENEUR'S DRAGON ENERGY

NOTABLE QUOTABLE:

"Find your dreams come true
And I wonder if you know
What it means, what it means
And I wonder if you know
What it means, what it means
And I wonder if you know
What it means to find your dreams."

- Kanye West - "Wonder"

Nearly all super successful people run around carrying a to do list, a notepad, or some type of note-taking device. They realize they might need to write down their next God-given idea. On the other hand, unsuccessful people never seem to have a pen available or a piece of paper nearby, and they struggle with constantly forgetting that "big idea" because they choose not to have the self-discipline to carry a writing device with them.

NOTABLE QUOTABLE

"Without a plan for your life, it is easier to follow the course of least resistance, to go with the flow, to drift with the current with no particular destination in mind. Having a definite plan for your life greatly simplifies the process of making hundreds of daily decisions that affect your ultimate success. When you know where you want to go, you can quickly decide if your actions are moving you toward your goal or away from it. Without definite, precise goals and a plan for their achievement, each decision must be considered in a vacuum. Definiteness of purpose provides context and allows you to relate specific actions to your overall plan."

- Napoleon Hill

ASK YOURSELF:

» What type of writing device will you keep on you at all times?

_____

_____

_____

» How will you arrange and file your notes so that you can find the information when you need it later?

_____

_____

_____

CHAPTER 31

DRAGON ENERGY POWER PRINCIPLE 31

LEARN TO EMBRACE THAT BAD THINGS ARE GOING TO HAPPEN TO YOU AND LEARN HOW TO DEAL WITH THEM

THE ENTREPRENEUR'S DRAGON ENERGY

My friend, you must learn to accept and embrace that bad things are going to happen to you. Trying to avoid all adversity is like trying to dodge the raindrops. As a young entrepreneur, I often thought that if I did everything correctly then nothing bad would happen to me. However, after less than 1 year in business with DJConnection.com, I had a person who I thought was a close friend, miss a wedding I had paid him to DJ, my childhood best friend and college roommate got killed in a car wreck, I had my equipment stolen and I had received countless rejections from event planners, brides to-be and prospective clients. When these bad things happened to me, I used to dwell on them, obsess on them and spend days asking myself, "Why me?" and, "Why would someone do this?" However, now at the age of 38, I realize that bad things will never stop happening to me and the best thing I can do is to believe for the best and prepare for the worst.

My younger self would not have bought insurance because I wanted to believe that, if I did everything right, my gear would never be stolen. The new me now embraces that fact that my equipment will be stolen and thus I buy insurance whenever possible. The old me would have believed that if I trained people correctly and really invested in them, they would never screw me. I know now that nearly everyone will eventually screw me and so I am always expecting and preparing for the worst-case scenario. My friend, blind optimism will not prevent bad things from happening to you.

In fact, when those bad things do happen to you, you must learn to prepare yourself emotionally, financially and logistically for these horrible things.

ASK YOURSELF:

» In what ways are you not preparing yourself emotionally for the bad things that will happen to you as an entrepreneur?

_____

_____

_____

» In what ways are you not preparing yourself financially for the bad things that will happen to you as an entrepreneur?

_____

_____

_____

» In what ways are you not preparing yourself logistically for the bad things that will happen to you as an entrepreneur?

_____

_____

_____

» In what ways could you have better handled a recent setback or adversity?

_____

_____

_____

CHAPTER 32

DRAGON ENERGY
POWER PRINCIPLE **32**

BE HUNGRY LIKE THE WOLF FOR THE KNOWLEDGE THEY DON'T TEACH IN COLLEGE

THE ENTREPRENEUR'S DRAGON ENERGY

NOTABLE QUOTABLE

"I'm hungry for knowledge. The whole thing is to learn every day, to get brighter and brighter. That's what this world is about. You look at someone like Gandhi, and he glowed. Martin Luther King glowed. Muhammad Ali glows. I think that's from being bright all the time, and trying to be brighter."

- Jay-Z (A rapper, entrepreneur, songwriter, and record producer. WIth 21 Grammy' Awards, he is one of the most awarded rappers of all-time. His individual net worth is reported by Forbes to now be over $900 million. However, if you combine the net worth of his wife Beyonce Knowles-Carter, with his own it is estimated that the couple is worth $1.16 billion)

Super successful people are very curious. They crave new, practical knowledge and are always looking to improve their skills. These people don't look to retire because they sincerely believe that their vocation is their calling. They are always trying to become the best version of themselves that they can possibly be. Unsuccessful people dislike work and the acquisition of practical knowledge. They would rather go on the campuses of academia to learn theories and concepts that they will never have to use because it's safer and easier. Degrees give them the false sense of accomplishment they need to feel good about themselves, although they are not actually doing anything but engaging in a giant game of memory.

NOTABLE QUOTABLE

"Rarely do we find men who willingly engage in hard, solid, thinking. There is an almost universal quest for easy answers and half-baked solutions. Nothing pains some people more than having to think."

- Martin Luther King Jr. (A Baptist minister and the most visible spokesperson and leader in the civil-rights movement beginning in the mid-1950s and continuing until his assassination in 1968.)

Much like using any muscle, thinking hard is hard work for your brain. Like any muscle, your mind will begin to atrophy when it is not used. You will begin to find it harder and harder to think on a deep level. Because most people can't stay off of their smartphone for 10 minutes to sustain a thought, let alone develop a skill, your ability to think deeply will truly separate you in this increasingly dumb and distracted society.

NOTABLE QUOTABLE

"In the future, the great division will be between those who have trained themselves to handle these complexities and those who are overwhelmed by them—those who can acquire skills and discipline their minds and those who are irrevocably distracted by all the media around them and can never focus enough to learn."

- *Robert Greene*

ASK YOURSELF:

» What skills do you need to improve on this year?

_____

_____

_____

» What new skills do you need to acquire this year?

_____

_____

_____

» What is one skill that would double your income if you mastered it?

_____

_____

_____

CHAPTER 33

DRAGON ENERGY
POWER PRINCIPLE 33

PUT YOUR
NAME ON IT

THE ENTREPRENEUR'S DRAGON ENERGY

NOTABLE QUOTABLE

"I'm serious about product. I'm dead serious about what I can create as an artist in this lifetime while I'm here."

- Kanye West

Super successful people are obsessed with quality, and because of that they do not hesitate to put their names on their products or to serve as the face of their company. My friend, as you invest more time studying the lives of super successful people you will discover in fact that only people who have a fervent obsession with their success every dominate financially.

NOTABLE QUOTABLE

"When you're a carpenter making a beautiful chest of drawers, you're not going to use a piece of plywood on the back, even though it faces the wall and nobody will see it. You'll know it's there, so you're going to use a beautiful piece of wood on the back. For you to sleep well at night, the aesthetic, the quality, has to be carried all the way through."

—Steve Jobs

NOTABLE QUOTABLE

"Do what you do so well that they will want to see it again and bring their friends."

- Walt Disney (The co-founder of the Walt Disney empire who was a pioneer of the American animation industry. He introduced several developments in the production of cartoons. As a film producer, Disney holds the record for most Academy Awards earned by an individual, having won 22 Oscars from 59 nominations. He was presented with two Golden Globe Special Achievement Awards and an Emmy Award, among other honors.)

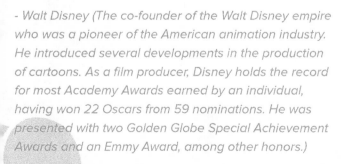

ASK YOURSELF:

» In what ways can you improve the quality of the service
you render or the products you make?

_____

_____

_____

» How can you take your reputation to the next level?

_____

_____

_____

CHAPTER 34

DRAGON ENERGY
POWER PRINCIPLE 34

BEWARE OF THE MOB MENTALITY AND TAKE ADVANTAGE OF THE HERD MENTALITY

THE ENTREPRENEUR'S DRAGON ENERGY

NOTABLE QUOTABLE

"Unite to win. Divide to conquer."

- President Donald J. Trump (The 45th President of the United States who earned his wealth and fame as a real estate developer, a best-selling author, a TV personality, the owner of the Miss USA and Miss Universe pageants, a golf course developer, and more.)

If you have ever run a team or spoken in front of a group of more than 50 people, you know the truth behind the quote, "Unite to win. Divide to conquer." When you are speaking to a large group of people, the crowd is quick to get overly negative or positive. Thus, if you have to deliver tough news, like firing someone or harsh criticism, you always want to deliver the tough message one-on-one or in a small group. However, if you need to praise someone, you would be wise to praise them in front of a large group of their peers. This will have a unifying and positive effect on the whole group.

NOTABLE QUOTABLE

"Consider the concept of group polarization. This means that a group of likeminded people reinforce one another's viewpoints. Group polarization strengthens of the opinions of each person in the group. In a study by French psychologists Serge Moscovici and Marisa Zavalloni, researchers asked participants some questions. First, researchers asked about their opinion of the French president. Second, they asked about their attitude toward Americans. The researchers then asked the participants to discuss each topic as a group."

- The Science Behind Why People Follow the Crowd - Rob Henderson - Psychology Today - March 24th, 2017

ASK YOURSELF:

» When was the last time that you experienced the wrath of the mob mentality because your failed to deliver constructive criticism in a small confidential and discreet way?

_____

_____

_____

» During your typical work week when should you "play to the crowd" and deliver positive news to a larger group of people?

_____

_____

_____

CHAPTER 35

DRAGON ENERGY POWER PRINCIPLE 35

LOATHE LAZINESS

NOTABLE QUOTABLE

"I can't relate to lazy people. We don't speak the same language. I don't understand you. I don't want to understand you."

- Kobe Bryant (Former professional basketball player. He played for 20 years in the National Basketball Association where he won 5 championships. He is the fourth highest-scoring NBA player by total career playoff points scored.)

I sincerely believe there is no cure for laziness - it ruins everything. No matter how great your idea is, your business will fail if you are lazy and casual about everything. Nearly all successful people are constantly labeled as "uptight," "anal," or "difficult to work with" because it irritates them when people show up late to meetings, make errors or overall deliver a half-assed effort. My friend, laziness is a habit that anyone can slip into. Diligence is a habit that you can develop through intentional effort. My hope and prayer for you is that if you are a lazy person with enough ambition to read this book. You will wake up and get serious about your life because laziness will kill your dreams.

ASK YOURSELF:

» In what areas of your life are you being lazy?

_____

_____

_____

» In what areas of your life are you being diligent?

_____

_____

_____

CHAPTER 36

DRAGON ENERGY POWER PRINCIPLE 36

STAND ALONE WHEN NEEDED

THE ENTREPRENEUR'S DRAGON ENERGY

More often than not, people will disagree with you once you begin to harness the power of "Dragon Energy." For example, I believe that a business exists to serve the owner, and the vast majority of people do not. Thus, the vast majority of business owners spend every waking hour of their lives running around trying to please every customer and every employee for every second of the day.

My friend, I know this might sound harsh, but I also believe that the vast majority of people are pretenders with big hopes who don't ever actually improve or change; they just want to appear as if they are getting better. The moment that you start holding yourself and other people accountable for delivering on the action items that have been discussed, you will begin to notice the vast difference between people with and without "Dragon Energy." To effectively communicate this message to my male employees, I have written the following text in the men's restroom on the walls with chalk:

"God is watching and I am too. Don't make me fire you."

— CLAY CLARK 2017

NOTABLE QUOTABLE

"I focus on educating you through facts, not fiction.
Teaching you Gold Standards like life before Nixon.
Executing on best practices and systems that work.
Is why I'm not Simon Sinek and often labeled as a jerk.
Four times I've done it, played the game and won it.
Four multi-million dollar companies later,
that's right I've done it.
Hard work plus no days off creates a dynasty.
With the only common denominator is there
would be nothing if you minus me.
You and I are not exceptional and
there is no such thing as luck.
But if you work six days per week
you won't get stuck."

- Clay Clark (2017)

ASK YOURSELF:

» What is something that you believe in that most people
   don't care about, and why?

_____

_____

_____

CHAPTER 37

DEMAND LOYALTY FROM YOUR TEAM

THE ENTREPRENEUR'S DRAGON ENERGY

There is a scenario I'll never forget because it blew my mind. In my own office, I had to fire a guy for sabotage-related issues, meaning that he was literally harming this particular business and putting everybody's jobs at risk. The day after I fired him, it was called to my attention that several of our employees were taking him out to eat as a sort of impromptu going-away party. My friends, this would be like inviting the Nazis over to celebrate a Bar Mitzvah, or inviting known Communists over to have a pep talk with our military before being deployed overseas to defend South Korea. This is would be like publicly inviting everyone to pee in the punch bowl before inviting everyone to enjoy that incredible wedding sherbet-punch hybrid people love so much. The moment that I saw this sort of disloyalty happening within our company, I immediately made the necessary plans to do some serious firing. Guess what we found when we fired these people. . . Much more sabotage-related activities were taking place than we thought.

venture capital firm Andreessen Horowitz. He previously co-founded and served as president and chief executive officer of the enterprise software company Opsware, which Hewlett-Packard acquired in 2007 for $1.6 billion in cash)

ASK YOURSELF:

» Who should be in your inner circle?

_____

_____

_____

» Who would you describe as being loyal and trustworthy?

_____

_____

_____

» Who is in your inner circle that needs to be removed?

_____

_____

_____

CHAPTER 38

DRAGON ENERGY
POWER PRINCIPLE 38

LEAVE THE DYSFUNCTIONAL PEOPLE BEHIND

NOTABLE QUOTABLE

"You make your first album, you make some money, and you feel like you still have to show face, like 'I still go to the projects.' I'm like, why? Your job is to inspire people from your neighborhood to get out. You grew up there. What makes you think it's so cool?"

- Jay-Z

I cannot stress how important it is to leave the idiots behind even if they happen to be your brother, sister, brother-in-law, sister-in-law, uncle, aunt, father-in-law, mother-in-law, father or mother. You need to move on, ESPECIALLY if they are family. So many people get trapped in a terrible life simply because they will not leave their negative, dream-killing, and dysfunctional family and friends behind.

ASK YOURSELF:

» Who is weighing you down and holding you back?

_____

_____

_____

» Who is passive-aggressively making it difficult for you to get things done?

_____

_____

_____

CHAPTER 39

DRAGON ENERGY
POWER PRINCIPLE **39**

USE ADVERSITY TO BECOME STRONGER

THE ENTREPRENEUR'S DRAGON ENERGY

NOTABLE QUOTABLE

"Now that that don't kill me, Can only make me stronger."

- *Kanye West*

Over time, as you develop the "Dragon Energy" mindset, you will begin to find that your best strengths are the result of constant struggle. Just as the mighty oak tree becomes almost indestructible as a result of fighting for its survival against the winds year after year, or a professional bodybuilder gains strength after pushing his body to its physical limits and to the point of pain during each workout, you, too, will gain strength as you begin to become more comfortable with dealing with heartache, rejection, setbacks, and betrayal.

NOTABLE QUOTABLE

"Being an entrepreneur is like eating glass and staring into the abyss of death."

- *Elon Musk*

ASK YOURSELF:

» In what areas are you too sensitive and too emotional?

_____

_____

» What areas of your business and life are you avoiding confronting and dealing with because you fear the pain and conflict involved in doing the necessary pruning needed for additional and sustainable growth?

_____

_____

CHAPTER 40

DRAGON ENERGY
POWER PRINCIPLE **40**

SHOOT UNTIL YOU HIT SOMETHING

THE ENTREPRENEUR'S DRAGON ENERGY

Whether I'm coaching Grammy award-winning clients like Charlie "Rocket" Jabaley or helping the founder of SKYY Vodka (Maurice Kanbar) market the 26% of the available commercial real estate in downtown Tulsa that he purchased, I carry the mentality that no one is going to out-hustle and out-grind us. In all cases and all situations, I am simply going to make a list of as many ideal and likely buyers as I can possibly think of, and then I am going to call, email, text, mail, and reach out to them by any means necessary until they cry, buy, or die.

If you want to achieve super success, you must develop the mindset to never allow what you can't do stop you from doing what you can do. In order to dominate as an entrepreneur, you must relentlessly pursue your goals with a sense of urgency that few understand. At the first sign of adversity most people stop, pause, question, lament, vent, feed their doubts, and begin to ask themselves questions like, "Does God really want me to do this?" or "I wonder if it's truly meant to be." As a business owner and an entrepreneur, I never ask myself these questions once I have committed to starting a project. I simply will not allow myself to stop taking massive action until I'm dead.

When I started DJ Connection I cold-called every venue in Oklahoma to convince them to allow me to DJ for free at their facility. This was my chance to demonstrate why DJConnection.com was the DJ and a wedding entertainment company they should be recommending to their customers. During this process I was rejected too many times to count, but I kept on grinding because I didn't care about my feelings and my emotions. I just cared about the results that I was seeking. If you want to achieve massive success in any calling, you must teach yourself to let go of how you feel or you will lose.

NOTABLE QUOTABLE

"Success seems to be connected to action. Successful people keep moving. They make mistakes, but they don't quit."

- Conrad Hilton (The iconic American hotelier and the founder of the Hilton Hotels chain)

Most humans want to celebrate successful people once they have achieved their massive success, but very few people seem interested in studying the lives of super successful people to determine what daily action steps they had to take to get there. If you are going to dominate as an entrepreneur, you must accept the truth that all people who have achieved massive success had to fight their way through rejection en route to the top.

For example, Conrad Hilton is now known as being the legendary founder of the Hilton Hotel chain, but did you know that after serving in the United States Army during World War I, Conrad initially wanted to buy a bank to make his fortune? However, he ended up buying the Mobley Hotel instead, which was located in Cisco, Texas. Why did he decide to buy this particular hotel, and how did he acquire the money needed to purchase it? This is the part of the story that no one ever seems to know or care about, and this is exclusively what I care about. Once I discover that somebody is super successful, my myopic focus immediately shifts to figuring out how they were able to achieve this success, and what adversities they faced during the pursuit of their ultimate achievements.

THE ENTREPRENEUR'S DRAGON ENERGY

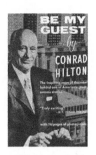

Conrad Hilton went through countless adversities that would have made the vast majority of people quit, but he kept on grinding, moving, and focusing on the action steps that he needed to take to turn his dreams into reality.

Conrad Hilton was born on Christmas Day of 1887. As a young man, Conrad learned business skills while working at his father's (Gus) general store located in Socorro County, New Mexico, which had actually been partially converted into a 10-room hotel. By the time Conrad was 23, he had already been working for his dad for 11 years.

While Conrad Hilton was serving in World War I for the United States Army, his father died in a car crash in France.

After returning from the war, Conrad was focused on buying a bank at the peak of the oil boom, and he had actually raised enough money from family, friends, and face-to-face networking to start a very small bank.

At the age of 32, Conrad had $5,011 of savings (which is equal to approximately $76,800.41 as of the beginning of 2019) and wasn't sure what to do next. His father's friend recommended that he move to Albuquerque to pursue his dreams of owning a bank. However, he did not make any progress.

Conrad was a man on a mission and could not be stopped. His father's friend then encouraged Conrad to move to Cisco, Texas to look for a bank to buy. However, while looking for a hotel to sleep in for the night, he encountered a hotel owner who was overwhelmed by the responsibilities of owning and operating a hotel. The owner believed that he was missing out on his opportunities in the oil industry because he was tied to hotel operations on a day-to-day basis. Conrad saw this as an opportunity and offered to buy the hotel from the man on owner-carried-financing terms, and much to his shock, the owner agreed. Thus, in 1919 at the age of 32, Conrad became the owner of the poorly managed Mobley Hotel in Cisco, Texas.

He used the profits from the Mobley Hotel to buy and build many hotels including the Dallas Hilton (which he opened in 1925), the Abilene Hotel (in 1927), and the Waco Hotel (in 1928). By the time Hilton celebrated his 41st birthday, he had nine hotels including the new El Paso Hotel.

However, Conrad Hilton later remembered, "[After opening the El Paso Hilton] Nineteen days later the stock market crashed."

In 1939 at the age of 52, he was able to build his first hotel outside of Texas in Albuquerque, New Mexico which is now known as the Hotel Andaluz.

During the Great Depression, Hilton was consistently pushed near the point of bankruptcy, but he refused to quit.

To survive, he sold off percentages of his hotels, borrowed money from all of the family and friends that he could find. At one point he ended up living in his hotels to reduce his personal cost of living.

Despite his resilience, he ultimately lost several of the hotels that he had built or purchased, but he never quit or gave in.

During a time when most entrepreneurs would have quit, Hilton continued fighting and was eventually able to make the Hilton Hotel chain sustainably profitable again after the Great Depression ended in 1939. At his absolute financial low point when he was deeply in debt and found himself with a court judgment against him, Conrad cut out a picture of the recently constructed Waldorf-Astoria Hotel in New York. After fighting for years to actually earn enough cash to be able to afford a desk, he put the picture of the Waldorf-Astoria under the glass top of the desk to remind himself that dreams do come true if you don't quit.

Although this fact has been lost on most people, Conrad Hilton was nearly 50 years old before he was able to buy an actual hotel outside of the great state of Texas. Nearly all of Conrad's success took time. In fact, the negotiation to purchase the Stevens Hotel in Chicago—which was the world's largest hotel at the time—actually took six years to negotiate.

In 1954, at the age of 67, Conrad Hilton astounded many people in the financial world when he successfully purchased his main competitor's company, Statler Hotels, for $111,000,000.

NOTABLE QUOTABLE "Ten rules of successful living: 1) Find your own particular talent 2) Be big 3) Be honest 4) Live with enthusiasm 5) Don't let your possessions possess you 6) Don't worry about your problems 7) Look up to people when you can – down to no one 8) Don't cling to the past 9) Assume your full share of responsibility in the world 10) Pray consistently and confidently."

- Conrad Hilton

ASK YOURSELF:

» In what ways are you simply not taking enough shots, making enough sales calls, or taking enough action?

_____

_____

» What is causing you to hold back the level of your activity when you know deep down that nothing will work until you do?

_____

_____

CHAPTER 41

DRAGON ENERGY
POWER PRINCIPLE 41

NOBODY CARES ABOUT YOUR FEELINGS AND YOU SHOULDN'T EITHER

Bottom line, as an entrepreneur you get paid based on what you do, not on what you intend to do. When my Dad was dying of Lou Gehrig's Disease, some people called and expressed their concerns about how much I was working, which I appreciated, but our paying customers still wanted to get their haircuts (at EITRLounge.com). Thrive15.com subscribers still wanted to watch their video content, and the Make Your Life Epic Agency business coaching clients still wanted coaching and results that they were seeking. If I had called in sick for a year because I was "dealing with emotional issues," everything would have fallen apart. My friend, if you want to succeed at the next level then you just have to SHOW UP EVERY SINGLE DAY, even if you have a headache or are going through a divorce. People will say they care, but if they can't count on you, your customers will fire you and take their money somewhere else.

ASK YOURSELF:

» How are you letting your feelings stop you from doing what you need to do?

_____

_____

» What is the emotional story, excuse, and justification that you keep telling yourself every week that nobody cares about and is stopping you from taking the massive action that you know you need to take?

_____

_____

I care enough about you and your success to list out the following excuses that I could make for myself. Most of our society would agree that these excuses justify stagnancy. However, these are not valid excuses if you want to achieve massive success:

» I stuttered as a kid and I am afraid of public speaking.

» I don't have the money to start a successful business.

» My son was born blind.

» My best friend died in college.

» My dad died from Lou Gehrig's Disease (ALS).

» I'm just not inspired right now.

» I don't have the time to get things done.

» I have a head cold and it's hard for me to focus.

» Tomorrow is Christmas and I ran out of time.

CHAPTER 42

DRAGON ENERGY POWER PRINCIPLE 42

SEIZE
THE DAY

THE ENTREPRENEUR'S DRAGON ENERGY

NOTABLE QUOTABLE -

"If you have the opportunity to play this game of life, you need to appreciate every moment. A lot of people don't appreciate the moment until it's passed."

- Kanye West

My friend, every day is truly a gift and you must come to grips with the concept that we are ALL GOING TO BE DEAD SOON. When you are intentional about designing and living each day as though it is your last, you can get a lot accomplished in one year. When I was 19 years old, my friend was killed, I got married to the love of my life (Vanessa Clark), and I got kicked out of college in the span of 12 months.

NOTABLE QUOTABLE

"The time will never be just right. We must act now."

- Napoleon Hill

As the summer was winding down, my plan was going well. I had saved up almost $13,000, and I knew how I was going to spend every last dime of it. I don't remember the exact totals of what everything cost, but I do remember writing them all down in a red spiral notebook. I wrote something to the effect of:

» American DJ Mixer = $300.00

» American DJ Light Trussing = $75.00

» Amp = $600.00

» Denontm CD player = $450.00

» Light Bin = $10.00 (Etc..)

Once I added it all together, it appeared as though I would need a little over $10,000 to transform my DJ Connection dream into a reality. I was getting so close to creating my dream job that I could taste it. I could see myself in possession of all the equipment. I could visualize Vanessa saying yes and agreeing to marry me and there was nothing that was going to stop me. I had arranged for Vanessa to fly to the Minneapolis airport so that she could meet my family, and then we could drive back to ORU together in my new, incredibly gorgeous, maroon MPV minivan. My Dad had secured a call-forwarding service through a company called AnswerPhone (these guys are great) to serve as the voicemail for my new DJ service—since I was going to be in class when 80 percent of the calls were coming in—and the number they gave me was (918) 481-2010. I was pumped! I had a number. I was in the phonebook. I was somebody! (Sorry, Steve Martin, for shamelessly stealing your movie lines). So I did the most sensible thing that any young entrepreneur without money to advertise would do:

I hand-painted this new number all over the exterior of my maroon MPV. Yes, that is right, my friend. I hand painted the words "DJ Connection" and its phone number right on the side of my minivan in big, bright letters and numbers. Oh, it was sweet! Plus, because I earned a little more money than I had expected from working as a home health aid/bingo-caller/bellboy in a retirement community on Saturdays and Sundays—the two days that I wasn't working construction, so I treated myself to the purchase of a new stereo system for my van. I had an amplifier and a subwoofer installed, and they sounded great. When Vanessa flew into Minneapolis, I felt like a million bucks.

Over the years, I have discovered that there is a certain emotional high that follows the completion and successful achievement of audacious goals. It seems as though achieving small goals builds your faith in your ability to achieve larger goals. A positive cycle of achievement was quickly created because I was really getting after it.

I was experiencing a near-euphoric emotional high, and I could not wait to propose to Vanessa. BECAUSE I HAD THE CONFIDENCE FROM THAT POSITIVE ACHIEVEMENT, I HAD NO DOUBT THAT SHE WOULD SAY YES.

After her plane landed, it taxied into position, and I remember having to focus on not drooling in anticipation of being with her again. As I gazed out the large airport terminal windows looking intently to catch a glimpse of my dream woman, my heart (I think it was my heart) pounded hard with anxiety/love/pre-proposal jitters. My dad and brother were waiting with me because this was pre-9/11 and the aviation protocols allowed us to wait for her in the actual terminal.

As she walked down the jet bridge exiting the plane, she looked so tan, so exotic, so beautiful, so happy, and so incredible in her blue denim skirt and red top. She wore silver earrings and a silver bracelet that the family she had been a nanny for over the summer had given her. I wanted to find a judge and marry her right there, but I had some patience, just not enough to propose to her in the way I had planned.

After we picked up Vanessa, my dad (Thom) took my brother (Carson), Vanessa, and I all out to eat at Olive Garden. The whole time we sat there, I kept wishing I could propose. If I had brought the ring with me, I would have. That night when my mom and Vanessa were talking in the kitchen, again, I wanted to propose. I had an elaborate engagement proposal plan, like most guys do, but I determined that this plan had to go by the wayside. I was into the results-approach. So that night as Vanessa got ready for bed, I knocked on the door to the guest room (my brother's room), and I proposed to her. She took forever to answer, and I almost wet myself in anticipation, but eventually she said yes. Each second I waited seemed like an eternity.

"When Clay and I decided to get married, I remember Clay's mom, Mary, telling me something to the effect of, 'If you marry Clayton, you will never have a normal life.' I think that reinforced my decision."

— Vanessa Clark (my wife, my leader and the "Big Bird")

So my new fiancé, Vanessa, and I finally hopped into the custom, hand-painted MPV van, drove one hour east to Minneapolis through the endless barrage of small towns, and then embarked on the twelve-hour drive to Tulsa. I remember thinking, "This is my life. This is great! I am going to change to world! My fiancé is hot. Holy cow, I am about to spend a lot of money on DJ gear . . . Wow!"

That particular series of events, might have been the most exciting time of my life up until that point. Just knowing that we were literally driving into the future together, and that I was about to make my dreams a reality with the purchase of the DJ gear left me ecstatic. When Vanessa and I finally arrived at the Guitar Center, my excitement almost could not be contained. I walked into that store with confidence, knowing that I was going to walk out with nearly eight thousand dollars of pre-negotiated DJ gear, and that a business would be born that day. Long story short, we spent several hours having the Guitar Center folks round up all the gear as I conversed with Joey "Shake," our sales representative.

When it was finally time to load the van with all the new gear, it occurred to me that we were definitely not going to have enough room. After much Tetris-esque repositioning of the gear, Vanessa finally had to scrunch up in a ball to fit into the van because the gig rig that housed all of the rack-mounted gear was taking up the passenger seat. That was one of the first times that I had ever asked Vanessa to do something crazy on behalf of the DJ business, but it would not be the last. I could barely change gears because of all the protruding equipment surrounding us. It was "man law" perfect, and it was awesome. Imagine being surrounded by Christmas presents and the significant other of your dreams all at the same time—this is what it had felt like.

Down the road we went. We drove, and drove, and drove, and drove some more for good measure. Finally after completing the thirteen-hour drive from Minnesota to Oklahoma we arrived at the mini-storage that would be the home of DJ Connection for some time. From this storage unit, we would load and unload disc jockeys every weekend for a four-year period. Terry, the lady running the storage facility, met us that day. She kindly escorted us to storage number 708. This unit was as small as an average bedroom closet—and so was my budget—so it was a good fit. After unloading, we were off to the dorm rooms to unload our domestic supplies. Because I always had a lot of stuff, this was never a pleasant process. I was always acquiring new DJ apparatuses and various pieces of gear, so I had the most technologically geeked-out room on the ORU campus. If my resident advisers had allowed it, I would have also started side businesses enriching uranium, activating carbon, or exploring for gas within my dorm room as well.

I might be mixing up the sequence of events here, but I believe at this time I was assigned a new roommate by the name of Clinton Clark because Mark D. was taking a semester off. Clinton and I did not hit it off right away. It's not that I did not like him. We were basically just a match not made in heaven. I think he did not enjoy my company, and I, in turn, did not enjoy his. Despite the oddness of sharing similar names (Clayton Clark and Clinton Clark) we were only roommates for a couple days because of my odd habit of taking up 90 percent of the usable space with turntables, speakers, condenser mics, gig rigs, lights in need of repairs, and forty professional sports team jerseys. I think that this might have been tolerable, but I am pretty sure that the 3:00 A.M. to 9:00 A.M. recording sessions got to him after a while. Or maybe it was the oddness of my work-twelve-hours/sleep-four-hours philosophy. Anyway, Clinton, if you get around to reading this, I am sorry that I frustrated you, but I wouldn't change anything.

When it was all said and done, Clinton moved out and into a room with Dave McGlohon across the hall, and since Mark did not enroll that semester, I ended up having my own room to myself.

With a room to myself, I got to work. I would work eighteen hours per day when not in class, and ten hours per day if I was in class. I made banners, signs, flyers, t-shirts, dorm room highlight videos, recordings. . . and anything else that I could turn into a profit. It was during this time that I developed some of the very concepts and phrases that we still use today at DJ Connection. The concept for the logo was designed during this time, I refined my ability to record and produce music, I developed my belief in working with an intense sense of haste. During this period of my life, every day was like a sprint. I would wake up at 6:00 a.m. to lift weights with Eugene. I would start classes at 7:50a.m., and get out at 2:00p.m. At 3:30p.m. I would head to my job at the call center where I worked. During my shift, I would check my voicemail every few hours to make sure that no customers had called from my yellow pages ad.

My room became known as, "The room where that DJ guy can record you." Everyone knew I was the "DJ connection." Everyone knew what room I was in, and everyone wanted to see it. RA's warned me about theft and risk. Over the years, if I had a dollar for every time someone tried to warn me about my liability, fire hazard, and theft risks during my DJ career, then I certainly would have had enough money to buy all of the capital-sucking insurance that was recommended by the fear-mongering, negative Nancy types.

I loved the atmosphere of my individual dorm room, but I did not like the aura of the overall dormitory. I loved the chi I created in my room, and the overall aura it had. I loved that my walls were covered in posters and motivational sayings; I loved the artwork I cut out of magazines; I loved my room. I have actually re-created that creative environment in every office in which I have worked since. I cannot think or work in a vanilla, personality-free environment.

As the school year progressed, and as my income began to soar like an eagle due to all of the recording time I was logging at $35.00 per hour, the harder it became for me to take college seriously.

THE ENTREPRENEUR'S DRAGON ENERGY

I got into heated debates with Dr. Swails, my history professor—,as well as with my Old Testament professors and teaching assistants. I was frustrated with the lack of practicality in 90 percent of the subject matter I was required to learn. But, I also was amazed by other professors like Mr. Westcott, who went on to become a city counselor, who devoted their class time to only teaching practical knowledge. I began questioning the whole concept of college and the idea of studying things that have no practical application in my life. I started realizing that my level of compensation was only determined by my practical education, my reputation and the overall level of my determination.

I read *The New Imperialists* and quickly discovered that Bill Gates, Steve Jobs, and other top-level business people relentlessly pursued continual learning and skill training. However, I also learned that Bill Gates, Steve Jobs, Russell Simmons, and many of the other business leaders whom I admired never earned a college degree. I started openly debating, questioning, and wondering why we had to become Microsoft-certified if the man who invented Microsoft was not Microsoft-certified.

In between my debates about the validity of college and studying, I also spent much time recording, hanging out with Vanessa, marketing my personal DJ services, commissioning myself to produce the Covenant wing year-in-review video, working out each morning, eating yogurt, eating frozen Budget Gourmet brand 96-cent chicken panini dinners, going to Walmart, eating ungodly amounts of chicken at the ORU cafeteria, reading Newsweek magazine, crudely soundproofing my room using the mattresses in my dorm room, recording my own rap parodies, recording other rappers, drawing, attending chapel at ORU, and debating with anyone who would listen about the fraudulent messages of Eastman Curtis and Richard Roberts and the insincerity of many televangelists, and then . . . I had the opportunity to meet ADAM BAGWELL.

Recording Adam Bagwell . . . oh yes . . . recording Adam Bagwell . . . nothing was more fun to me at the time.

Now that I am married, nothing is more fun than attempting to create babies, but at the time, this was where it was. Adam Bagwell was this extremely skinny, white kid from Golden, Colorado, who could rap like he was born doing it. Up until that point, I had heard people rap and always thought, I could do better than that; that was okay; or that requires no talent. But with Adam, I did not have those thoughts. He was great. He could change the emphasis on nearly any word or phrase to make it rhyme. When he rapped, he had a synonym for nearly every word readily available to make the rhyme phrase work without compromising the meaning.

Since everybody at school knew I rapped, recorded, and DJ-ed, and everyone on Kingsmen's dorm floor knew Adam's rapping skills were incredible, it was just a matter of time before Adam and I found each other. I kept hearing people say, "When are you and Adam going to hook up and record something?" I did not know who he was, but I was kind of beginning to look forward to meeting him. With a knock on my room 2416 metal door, the funkiest white kid I had ever met, Adam Bagwell, entered my life.

Both of us went through school at Oral Roberts University, we found an oasis of creativity behind the microphone and recording. It was almost as though the microphone represented a secret pathway into the Narnia of recording. Adam and I recorded jams for the ORU Battle of the Bands and for others just because. We found that we worked well together and that we never limited the creativity of the other person. I recorded the "Ford Escort Song," (available for download on the www.djconnectiontulsa.com) a tribute to my late 1989 Ford Escort and my first DJ ride. Adam recorded Christian and positive-minded rap songs. I recorded off-the-wall love songs for my fiancée. And then late one night (all night) we recorded it; we recorded "ORU SLIM SHADY."

This parody was and still is the ultimate ORU campus song. This song brought excessive amounts of heat upon us because it brought the broadly (but quietly) held belief that Lindsay and Richard Roberts were allegedly corrupt into campus conversations among the students.

To be fair, the song was caustic, and to be fair, it was funny; but it did get me in a lot of trouble.

Because people liked the song, and because we were attending college during the year 2000, the song spread quickly via the Napster file-sharing program. This song began to grow at a viral pace after a few of our friends "borrowed it" and put it online. I will probably never know who put the song on Napster, or who put the song on every student's campus voicemail, but I do know that this song made me instantaneously infamous at ORU and made me forever synonymous with the "ORU SLIM SHADY."

Before this audio sensation made its way across campus via CD, e-mail, and the school's voicemail system, Adam was long gone. When he transferred to Colorado Christian University, the song's popularity reached its peak. Around the time of the song's 10,000th download off of Napster, I was the only one left at ORU to answer for the song's content . . . which I actually enjoyed doing. For whatever reason, I actually get a big thrill out of having confrontations with people when I know that I am right. At the end of the day, this little audio gem worked tirelessly spreading its way around campus until eventually I was asked to leave the school by the dean of men, Dean B.

Sometime before the song reached its absolute pinnacle in popularity, my life changed. It was late in the evening, maybe around midnight. Just like any other night when returning to ORU past curfew after one of my DJ shows, I signed in at the front desk with Dan the bulky night security guy. I again risked my life by hopping on the old-school elevator in our dormitory and hit the 4 button to take me up to Covenant. As I rode up, nothing felt different, and I looked forward to a night of good sleep since I was exhausted.

When the elevator doors opened, I stepped out of the old-school, linoleum-style "retro-vator," and I turned right to round the corner on the way to my dorm room.

As I rounded the corner, I finally felt something different in the air, and I noticed that nearly every man on our wing was sitting in the hall. Some guys were crying, some guys were silent, and others tried to console each other. I figured at this point that possibly the wing had been disbanded, which was always a constant threat from the deans who did not appreciate our attention to detail when planning wing-initiation ceremonies, nude dorm marches, or rival mascot stealing nights.

As I walked past twenty-five of the greatest guys on earth and went to room 2416, my lifelong buddy and the Spartan-looking Adam Guthmann grabbed my shoulder in a fatherly manner and asked if he could come into my room. He said, "I don't know how to tell you this, so I am just going to tell you. Mark (my best friend growing up and my current roomate) is dead. He was killed in a car accident. We didn't know how to reach you so . . ."

At that point, I quit listening. I am pretty sure that somebody suggested that we ought to pray. I'm not positive, but I think someone did. I do recall not wanting to pray. I was never really one to pray about anything good or bad. I don't know why that was. I guess I just believed that God ultimately did what He wanted to do, and we really didn't have much say in His ultimate game plan. I figured that I should just do the best I could do, and if He stopped or helped me along the way, that was fine. Even if it wasn't fine, there wouldn't be much of a point arguing with God.

The more Adam talked, the more I lost touch with reality. My mind frantically bounced around with a mixture of memories, sorrow, thoughts, doubts, ideas, hope, and could haves. All of the negative thoughts soon vanished, and my short-term mission occurred to me. I felt a need to do something, so without hesitation, I grabbed my keys and hopped into the hand-painted, maroon MPV and headed over to Mark's parents' house. I never stopped to think that it was after midnight and that Mark would not be there regardless of how fast I drove to his parents' house.

When I pulled in the driveway of Rich and Pam DePetris's house in Sand Springs, my emotions finally got the best of me. I burst into tears, losing complete control to the point that I could not drive. I just sat there in the driveway, hitting my steering wheel and crying. I sat mourning and hoping that God would somehow do a New Testament-style miracle and bring my best friend back to life. It's funny how even now years later, I often still pray for that same miracle. I always pray that God would restore him like in the story of Lazarus. I am sure that if He did, someone would call him a demon, but I now know that God has that kind of power. After all, He created the Earth. For some odd reason, God has not answered this prayer. I think it's probably because of some sin in my life. *(Actually, I don't think of any of that.)* Spiritually, I just no longer think about it because thinking of Mark's death is too painful. I just trust that Mark is where he is supposed to be for a reason.

I don't remember when I told Vanessa (my fiancée at the time) about Mark's death. I don't remember how she reacted to it. But I do know that I felt tremendous emptiness in my heart, that Mark, my friend who had encouraged me to get married so young and the man who was going to be the best man in our wedding was gone (Just to clarify, Joe Casey made a fine best man, and he would have been the best man had it not been for Mark's relationship with me). Had I listened to other people, I would not have been engaged at all. Mark was my encourager; Mark was one of the sparks that lit the DJ Connection passion flame.

In the following days leading up to Mark's funeral, I changed. Mark's parents changed. Many people's worlds changed. Mark's funeral bore witness to his character and his life's impact as over 500 people who he had somehow touched attended his service. It was incredible to see the outpouring of love displayed. It's sad to me that Mark never got a chance to see this overwhelming impact and love until after he died (he saw it from an aerial perspective).

The entire wing of Covenant came to support the DePetris family, and for that, I will always be grateful. As I gave the eulogy for my best friend before Mark's peers and family, the men of Covenant seemed to nudge me along with their prayers and presence. It is amazing how at that time, for the first time, I was completely unafraid of the audience I was speaking to while in a public speaking situation.

I was unafraid of their reactions because I knew what I was saying was divinely inspired glimpses into the life of a great man . . . Mark DePetris.

I remember almost losing it once because I simply could not hold back my tears any longer. I had tried to make his eulogy uplifting and humorous, but I just could not fight back the tears. At that point, I looked up to the back of that Baptist church in Sand Springs, Oklahoma, and there I caught a glimpse of my friend and wing mate Adam Guthmann. He made eye contact with me in a way that said so much. With his eyes he said, "You can do it, Clayton." With his eyes he said, "I love you as a brother. And you can do this. You will do this. Now, quit crying and do it!" I will always remember Adam being there and looking me in the eye to guide me through the closing remarks of the hardest public speaking gig that I have ever had.

From that point on, I never battled uncontrollable stage fright again. Growing up, I used to struggle severely with stuttering. Every time I would misspeak or get stuck on a word, this overwhelming feeling of anxiety would take over. Thus, whenever I was asked to speak as part of a church play or any public event, those overwhelming feelings of anxiety would return, and I would simply refuse to speak publicly even if it meant getting into trouble with my teachers. However, after giving Mark's eulogy, I have no longer been overtaken with those feelings of anxiety when speaking publicly. Like everyone else, I do get nervous with anticipation. The adrenaline still gets pumping, but I no longer fear with the life-and-death intensity that I once did speaking in front of an audience.

I do sincerely value the opinions of people who have experience in the particular areas that I work in, and I do value the opinions of those whom I consider to be authorities on their areas of experience. But the random opinions of most people do not affect me anymore; they have no traction with my mind or soul. Albert Einstein said it best when he said, "Great minds have often encountered violent opposition from mediocre minds."

**AN UNBIASED VOICE OF SANITY

THE ENTREPRENEUR'S DRAGON ENERGY

"Clayton has always displayed a large vocabulary but he lacked the ability to express it. Having had a severe stammer for which he was teased mercilessly, Clayton had a tendency to shy away from any event in which he would have to be in front of people. Our church had an annual Christmas program in which the younger children sang. Clayton would go to all the practices. He even appeared to enjoy practicing with his friends.

But . . . on the day of the program, he would yell, scream, cry, roll on the floor; anything to not go on stage. This didn't happen just once. It was an annual occurrence guaranteed to happen just as the children were walking through the door to go onstage. Getting on stage was a fate akin to death for him, even if he didn't have a speaking role.

Fast-forward twelve years. Clayton had a boom box, a set of CDs, and a borrowed microphone plugged into the middle school gymnasium sound system. There were a couple hundred kids following his lead as he got them to dance and have a good time. One parent said, 'Your son really has a gift for entertaining. You must really be proud of him.'

Who? I thought. 'He looks like my son. He sounds like my son. But after having seen my son at Christmas programs, I think he has been kidnapped by aliens and replaced with an android that looks like him.'

The truth is that I am proud of him. But I am also amazed, if not just down-right shocked."

— Thom Clark (my dad)

I have never been one to value the mindless opinions of most people to begin with, but after Mark's death, I no longer spent any of my time trying to please anyone who I do not sincerely care for, or whose favor I do not seek. It was through Mark's death that I was taught how to live life. Thank you, Mark. Without Mark, I know that I would have been successful, but I would not have begun to scratch the surface of my potential at a young age. It changed my outlook on life. I seized each day with a new level of passion that I still carry to this day. I view life as gift, and each day that I get access to is a true blessing.

After Mark passed, I awoke each day even more impatient for what life had in store for me. For I knew that I was definitely not guaranteed anything. It was with this new attitude that I really started to pursue my passions, my goals, and my plans to achieve them. Off to class at ORU I went. Each day as I sat in Humanities, Government, and Quantitative Literacy listening to my professors, I became more and more sure that I, and most of the students in these classes, were wasting our time studying and memorizing general pieces of knowledge. What we really needed to learn was practical and applicable knowledge.

During one particular class (Humanities), the class lecture grew so theoretical that I remember jotting down notes resembling the following thought process: If I sit here for four years of my life, and I will probably only live to be 82 or so, then I will have spent 4.8% of my life here doing nothing. Whereas, if I spent even three months studying and marketing myself as a DJ, I could become successful using only about .05% of my life. If I were to spend my time studying only things that I cared about, I would be much more interested in them, and then I would not be listening to professors talk about the Justinian empire and how to plot a sloping line (no offense to the Justinian empire or those who enjoy graphing sloping lines).

It was thoughts like these that made it harder and harder to endure lectures about business from professors who had never owned a business. I wanted to hear lectures, but I wanted to hear them from business owners. Armed with thoughts like these, I mowed through tests, aced Government and other courses that mattered. Theoretical classes that involved truth tables started to become so unbearable that I started to feel the need to debate the validity of these classes with my professors. They always responded in upset, irritated tones as they attempted to defend the purpose of their job they were not passionate about. I grew more and more anxious to get on with my life. I became so frustrated with the slow pace of college that

I debated simply dropping out of college altogether. I was ready to leave the college yesterday when the deans called me into their dark wood-paneled offices of discipline and reprimand to answer for the "ORU SLIM SHADY" content. As the deans asked me questions, I did everything that I could to verbally and physically communicate that I was thoroughly unapologetic about the song's content, and I was defiant to the end.

What made the situation extra fun was that they knew the songs lyrics, untactful but accurate, spoke about the feelings that many students had toward the administration. The school was operating with a blatant double standard. Athletes and students of privilege were not forced to adhere to the Honor Code (the Honor Code was ORU's agreement that every student had to sign stating the rules of the school and the moral conduct that is expected of all students choosing to enroll in the college) while other students were forced to follow it. Richard Roberts had his own jet and lived a lavish lifestyle financed by university debt, while average families and students were expected to give everything they could to the ministry for the "good of the kingdom."

The Deans talked about how they valued this Honor Code so much, but it was apparent to me that these men honored that code the way that rednecks who fly the Confederate flag honor their country.

They did not really "honor" the code; they just referenced the code when it was convenient to support their way of thinking and inconsistent rulings on student-life issues. However, when the code was not convenient, they simply chose not to reference it (for the record, if you have a Confederate flag flying on your flagpole, we need to talk).

In my opinion, the Deans were apologists for the Lindsay and Richard Roberts personal expense foundation (as witnessed in the 2008 lawsuit launched by former ORU professors against Lindsay and Richard). The Deans definitely did not like that this song exposed their bosses for being the "alleged" fraudulent, lying plunderers of the ministry that they were. Later, all of America witnessed Richard's fraudulence before "God told Richard to resign" (which is Richard's code language for: my lawyers have pointed out to me that there is no way in hell I have even the smallest chance of beating these lawsuits. Holy crap, I am definitely seeing my misdeeds hitting the fan. I think I will resign if the school promises to drop all charges).

During my 2000 fallout with the administration, these Deans never seemed to have any problem with Lindsay and Richard's "alleged" strong-arming of the university to give scholarships to students whom they liked who had only scored a twelve on their ACTs. They did not seem to have any issues with Richard using his students' required chapel time as his chance to fleece the entire student body for yet another monetary "seed faith gift" to their ministry, so they could "allegedly" fire up their personal jet one more time en route to the Atlantis resorts in the Bahamas. These Deans never seemed too concerned that Lindsay would title her sermons with such catchy phrases as, "Get the Hell Out of Your Life." These Deans never seemed to notice they were promoting hypocrisy by endorsing Lindsay and Richard Roberts and by standing behind them no matter how out-of-control they allegedly got.

**AN UNBIASED VOICE OF SANITY

As of this date (1/23/09), if anyone asked me if I would encourage my child to attend ORU, I would give an emphatic YES. My best friends and deepest relationships are all the results of attending ORU. I now feel a deep affection for my alma mater. If asked the same question between 1993 and 2007, I would have answered an equally emphatic NO. Clayton attended ORU during the 1993-2007 timeframe. I am even more proud of him for learning from adversity and standing up for his principles, even when those in leadership did not.

— Thom Clark (my dad and an ORU graduate)

THE ENTREPRENEUR'S DRAGON ENERGY

**HUGE DISCLAIMER:

Anyway . . . long story short . . . they kicked me out of ORU for "selling
and distributing a song" on campus. I actually recorded my exit interview
with the Deans without them knowing, and I will sometimes listen to it
when I need some extra motivation (as if being taunted for stuttering and
losing my best friend were not motivation enough). Being kicked out of
college forced me to mature quickly. And I did. With my back against the
wall, I moved into the Fountain Crest apartments with help from my mom
and dad who had to co-sign for me. I cannot thank my parents enough for
helping me out and believing in me. It would have killed my spirit to move
back "up north" to Minne-snow-ta to live in a land where the mosquito
is the state bird, the winter is dangerously cold, and basketball, baseball,
and football come in fourth, fifth, and sixth in popularity behind hunting,
fishing, and casino gaming.

With the help of my fiancé, Vanessa, I sustained myself by eating bagels
from the ORU cafeteria. Vanessa and I got married later that spring on
a Sunday in May (so that many of our college friends and family would
still be able to attend before they flew back to their hometowns for the
summer). Our wedding was beautiful, and our future was bright.

NOTABLE QUOTABLE

"Knowledge without application is meaningless."

- Thomas Edison (The founder of GE and the man credited with having invented the modern light bulb, recorded audio, and recorded video.)

Don't let this chapter have less lasting meaning and overall impact on your life than of those super-intense people who scream at you as they pass your car while they drive by yelling and pleading for you to close your gas tank (because you accidentally left it open). Fill out the following form before moving on to the next chapter. You just might learn something:

Write down and describe the biggest setback that you have dealt with in your life up to this point (examples: death of a loved one, stuttering, getting kicked out of college, being unable to find matching socks, etc).

» What life lesson did you learn from this setback?

_____

_____

NOTABLE QUOTABLE

"Nothing in life is promised except death."

- Kanye West

Whether you are a hardcore, far-right Republican or a super motivated, left-of-center Democrat, we all know that we will be dead soon. I would encourage you to always view every day as though it were your last. In fact, having interviewed nearly 500 of the world's most successful people during my lifetime, I can tell you that this is the mindset of every super successful person that I've interviewed.

THE ENTREPRENEUR'S DRAGON ENERGY

Although Mahatma Gandhi and I could have never agreed on Jesus, we could have both agreed that he was correct when he said, "Live as if you were to die tomorrow. Learn as if you were to live forever."

ASK YOURSELF:

» If you knew that you were going to be dead within the next five years what would you start doing?

_____

_____

» If you knew that you were going to be dead within the next five years what would you stop doing?

_____

_____

» If you knew that you were going to be dead within the next year what would you start doing?

_____

_____

» If you knew that you were going to be dead within the next year what would you stop doing?

_____

_____

CHAPTER 43

DRAGON ENERGY
POWER PRINCIPLE **43**

BLOW YOUR
OWN HORN

THE ENTREPRENEUR'S DRAGON ENERGY

NOTABLE QUOTABLE

"Show me someone without an ego,
and I'll show you a loser."

- President Donald J. Trump

From my experience working as a business coach, it seems like in general the scammers who don't have a real product or service are very effective at self-promotion. Conversely, the people who have a real product or service are the ones who tend to struggle with sharing the problems they can solve or why we should buy their products or services. My friend, history favors the bold. Marketing is about nothing more than getting your product or service in front of your ideal and likely buyers in a memorable and remarkable way.

NOTABLE QUOTABLE

"If you're remarkable, it's likely that some people won't like you. That's part of the definition of remarkable. Nobody gets unanimous praise—ever. The best the timid can hope for is to be unnoticed. Criticism comes to those who stand out."

- Seth Godin

If you want to succeed in this world of entrepreneurship, you have to work diligently to become truly great at something. However, becoming great at something is only 50% of the battle.

Once you create a great product or service that world needs, you must also become great at selling your solutions both loudly and proudly.

NOTABLE QUOTABLE

"You desire but do not have, so you kill. You covet but you cannot get what you want, so you quarrel and fight. You do not have because you do not ask God. 3 When you ask, you do not receive, because you ask with wrong motives, that you may spend what you get on your pleasures."

- James 4:2–3

NOTABLE QUOTABLE

"Half the battle is selling music, not singing it. It's the image, not what you sing."

- Rod Stewart (The famous British rock singer and songwriter who has had 16 top ten singles in the United States and four singles that have reached the #1 spot on the Billboard Hot 100. Throughout his career, he has sold over $150 million in albums and singles)

ASK YOURSELF:

» In what ways are you being too humble about marketing your products and services?

_____

_____

» In what ways are you underselling your services, your activities, and your skills to your ideal and likely buyers?

_____

_____

» In what ways are you undercharging for your services
and products?

NOTE: Never take advantage of your customers, but also never let your

customers take advantage of you. In most cases, healthy business operates at a

sustainable net 20% profit margin after paying all expenses and all employees

(and yes this includes paying yourself too).

CHAPTER 44

BECOME SOLUTION-MINDED AND FUTURE-FOCUSED

THE ENTREPRENEUR'S DRAGON ENERGY

NOTABLE QUOTABLE

"I don't care about three years ago... I don't care about two years ago. I don't care about last year. The only things I care about is this week."

- Tom Brady (Drafted in the sixth round by the New England Patriots in 2000, Tom is one of only two players in entire history of the NFL to have won five Super Bowls (along with defensive player Charles Haley). However, he is the only player to have won all five Super Bowls with just one team.)

The most successful people I have been around are constantly talking about the future and turning their big plans into reality. Almost universally, perpetually poor people will talk about their past weekend, what they did in high school, or things that happened twenty years ago. In many cases, they actually start to believe that their best years are behind them and that their time to achieve has passed. All of the super successful people that I have interviewed over the years love to stay busy creating their futures, getting things done, and choosing not to lament over past mistakes. They tend to operate in the following rhythm and flow:

» Define - Define what you think will solve the problem.

» Act - Take action with Big, Overwhelming, Optimistic Momentum. (BOOM)

» Measure - Measure the results of your activities accurately and objectively.

» Refine - Refine your processes and action steps as required, but don't stop moving forward.

NOTABLE QUOTABLE

"In times of great stress or adversity, it's always best to keep busy, to plow your anger and your energy into something positive."

- Lee Iacocca (The former CEO of Chrysler responsible for leading their turn-around and keeping the company in business.)

Successful people simply don't spend much of their time lamenting their past mistakes. They aren't paralyzed by fear or doubts like most people. If you want to take your life to the next level, you too must learn this skill.

ASK YOURSELF:

» In what ways are you not consistently acting solution-minded and future-focused?

_____

_____

_____

_____

» In what areas of your life are you lamenting about things that happened in the past instead of keeping your mind focused on the future?

_____

_____

_____

_____

CHAPTER 45

DRAGON ENERGY POWER PRINCIPLE 45

DON'T ALLOW OPINIONS, DISTRACTIONS, B-PLAYERS, DOUBTERS, AND HATERS SLOW YOU DOWN

THE ENTREPRENEUR'S DRAGON ENERGY

As someone with serious amounts of "Dragon Energy," I can assure you that very few things irritate me like a bureaucrat who refuses to take action. They want to gather endless amounts of opinions, surveys, and feelings until they have come up with every possible reason to do nothing, to say nothing, and to be nothing because it may offend someone, or it's not the perfect timing, etc. It's important to think about things before we do them, but if you want to succeed as an entrepreneur, you simply cannot have too many slow-moving bureaucrats around you, or nothing will ever get done.

As an entrepreneur with "Dragon Energy," you understand that lazy people typically resent successful people because they are getting outworked by them. Therefore, they tend to focus their conversations on criticizing the people who they can't compete with because of their lack of self-discipline.

ASK YOURSELF:

» Who are you allowing to slow you down in your business?

_____

_____

_____

» What B-players are killing your dreams by constantly questioning why they need to do something and whether it's really "their highest and best use"?

_____

_____

_____

» Who are the doubters in your life and how can you minimize the amount of time that you have to spend with these exciting individuals?

_____

_____

_____

» Who are the haters in your life?

_____

_____

_____

» How can you minimize the amount of time that you must spend with doubters, haters, distracters, and unproductive people?

_____

_____

_____

_____

FUN FACT:

I actually built a wall around my house to keep the doubters, haters, distracters, and unproductive people out.

CHAPTER 46

DRAGON ENERGY POWER PRINCIPLE 46

DON'T ALLOW LACK OF EXPERIENCE TO STAND IN THE WAY

THE ENTREPRENEUR'S DRAGON ENERGY

When you have "Dragon Energy," success will become easy. You will find yourself wanting to dominate and explore multiple industries and different business opportunities. But remember to proceed with caution here; you don't want to get spread so thin that everything you touch turns to failure.

ASK YOURSELF:

» In what ways are you spreading yourself too thin as an entrepreneur?

_____

_____

_____

» What are business opportunities that you would like to explore within the next five years?

_____

_____

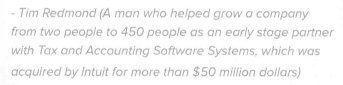

» How much time and financial freedom do you need to be earning from your first business before you can realistically work on your next project or your future expansion project?

_____

_____

_____

CHAPTER 47

DRAGON ENERGY POWER PRINCIPLE 47

PUSH THROUGH THE PAIN

THE ENTREPRENEUR'S DRAGON ENERGY

NOTABLE QUOTABLE

"After the first day of practice, there's not one guy who's playing at 100 percent or who feels great. Sometimes, getting up in the morning and brushing your teeth is the hardest part of the day—it just hurts."

- Tom Brady

People who have chosen to embrace "Dragon Energy" take pride in not missing games, days of work, or anything that they have committed to being a part of. My friend, every successful person that I know is obsessed with "keeping the streak alive" and being known as Mr. or Ms. Dependable. Super successful people pride themselves on pushing through the pain and having zero sympathy for themselves. This, my friend, is the spirit of the dragon at its finest.

NOTABLE QUOTABLE

"Be the pig at breakfast not the chicken. You must be willing to give your life for victory and not merely just some of your effort."

- Doctor Robert Zoellner (The founder of Doctor Robert Zoellner and Associates, the Z66 Auto Auction, A to Z Medical, Dr. Zzz's Sleep Center, an early stage investor and former board member of Regent Bank, etc)

Some of the most obvious examples of this are found in professional sports. The legendary Green Bay Packers, New York Jets, and Minnesota Vikings quarterback Brett Favre set the National Football League record for having played in 297 consecutive regular season games (321 including the playoffs).

During his senior year while playing college football at Southern Mississippi, Brett Favre got into a car accident that involved flipping his car. As a result of the numerous injuries that Brett experienced, he had to have 30 inches of his intestine removed. Within just five weeks, he was back on the field playing football. However, during his career, he played through the following injuries and more to "keep the streak alive."

In 2003, Brett broke his thumb but continued to push through the pain and played every single game during the season while playing for the Green Bay Packers.

During the 2006 season, Brett played most of the season with a severely injured ankle that ultimately required surgery after the season was over.

» A first-degree shoulder separation.

» A deep thigh bruise.

» A severely bruised left hip.

» A severely sprained left ankle.

» Having the wind knocked out of him, coupled with coughing up blood.

» A sprained right thumb.

» Tendinitis in his right elbow.

» A left mid-foot sprain.

» A sprained lateral collateral ligament in his left knee.

» A softball-sized bruise on his left hamstring.

» A mild concussion.

» A sprained right hand.

» An injured ulnar nerve in his right elbow.

» Bone spurs in his left ankle.

» Torn right biceps.

» A pulled groin.

» A stress fracture on his left ankle coupled with an avulsion fracture on his calcaneus.

» A sprained sternoclavicular joint in his right shoulder.

THE ENTREPRENEUR'S DRAGON ENERGY

FUN FACTS:

Not only did Hall of Fame baseball player and Baltimore Oriole Cal Ripken, break Lou Gehrig's streak of playing in 2,130 games consecutive games without missing a streak, but he also went on to play for 2,632 games without missing a game.

During a team photo shoot for the 1996 All-Star Game, Chicago White Sox pitcher Roberto Hernandez slipped and broke Ripken's nose. Ripken played in that All-Star Game and then for the Orioles two days later when the regular season resumed.

Ripken hit a home run in the game in which he tied Gehrig's record, and a home run in the game in which he broke Gehrig's record.

NOTABLE QUOTABLE

"I tumbled into the stands at Yankee Stadium and banged my shin onto a concrete wall," he says. "When I took my uniform off, I had a big gash there and had to have stitches put in before I went to the next city.
The hardest injury to play through was a herniated disk in 1997, two years after the record was broken. Some people said I was selfish, but we were a good team that year and beat the Yankees from the first day of the season to the last. The doctors told me I'd be out six weeks until the swelling could go away and the pain would go away. But I had waited a long time to be part of a team that was winning, so I asked myself whether I could do any serious damage if I was able to play. Somehow, I was able to perform. But I had no relief from pain for six weeks."

"There were a bunch of injuries that were tough. After the record was broken, I played through a herniated disc in my back in 1997. At that point, we had Eric Davis go down. He was diagnosed with cancer. Robbie Alomar got hurt that year and he was on the disabled list. And we were ahead of the Yankees, and the Yankees were pushing us a little bit. And I almost felt compelled to say, OK, I've been playing to want to be on a winner all this time. We're really good, and I don't want to miss this."

"For me, the streak happened as an extension of a simple approach to go out and be responsible to my team, to play. The only pressure I ever felt came within a season of my breaking the record when critics in the media suddenly became advocates. All of a sudden, a huge population of people thought it was important for me to break the record."

- Cal Ripken, Jr. (Hall of Fame baseball player for the Baltimore Orioles)

ASK YOURSELF:

» How often have you called in sick when you really weren't that sick?

» In what ways have you been really weak and have simply chosen not to show up to work in the past year?

CHAPTER 48

DRAGON ENERGY
POWER PRINCIPLE 48

TALK BIG
AND DELIVER
BIGGER

THE ENTREPRENEUR'S DRAGON ENERGY

My friend, throughout my life I have personally sat down and interviewed NBA MVP, two-time NBA Champion, and 2-time Gold Medalist turned entrepreneur and investor—David Robinson; the public relations consultant of choice for Nike, Prince, Michael Jackson, President Bush, President Clinton, Nancy Kerrigan, George Michael, and Charlton Heston—Michael Levine; the pastor of the largest protestant church in America—Craig Groeschel; and countless other top level entrepreneurs. I can tell you that each and every one of them cast a big vision, but they deliver even bigger results.

ASK YOURSELF:

» During the past year, in what ways have you failed to deliver up to the level of your own hype?

_____

_____

_____

» During the past year, in what ways have you delivered over and above what you have promised?

_____

_____

_____

CHAPTER 49

DRAGON ENERGY
POWER PRINCIPLE **49**

VIEW FAILURE AS A PREREQUISITE TO SUCCESS

THE ENTREPRENEUR'S DRAGON ENERGY

NOTABLE QUOTABLE

"I will not lose, for even in defeat, there's a valuable
lesson learned, so it evens up for me."

- Jay-Z

Many people get very emotional about rejection and process it like an
arrow shot directly at them that has pierced their heart. However, all of
the super successful people that I have interviewed throughout my life
view failure very differently. They somehow found a way to view every
failure or setback as something that carries an equal or greater benefit via
a learning opportunity. In fact, super successful people view failure as a
prerequisite to the ultimate achievement of their success. Because of that
they are not discouraged in the least by the rejections and adversities that
they encounter en route to their success.

NOTABLE QUOTABLE

"Every adversity, every failure, every heartache carries
with it the seed of an equal or greater benefit."

- Napoleon Hill

ASK YOURSELF:

» How have you been rejected during the past year?

_____

_____

_____

» What have you learned as a result of these rejections?

_____

_____

_____

CHAPTER 50

DRAGON ENERGY
POWER PRINCIPLE 50

EMBRACE THAT FOR EVERY CARROT THERE MUST BE A STICK

THE ENTREPRENEUR'S DRAGON ENERGY

NOTABLE QUOTABLE

"There's an old German proverb to the effect that "fear makes the wolf bigger than he is," and that is true."

- President Donald J. Trump

For years, I tried in vain to motivate my team using only "positive reinforcement" because that's what I was taught by the failing public school system. However, over time I discovered that nearly everybody needs both the carrot and the stick to motivate them to achieve greatness.

NOTABLE QUOTABLE

"All human behavior is determined by escaping discomfort."

- Nir Eyal (Best-selling author of Hooked and Thrivetime Show Podcast guest.)

NOTABLE QUOTABLE

"Public hangings are teaching moments. Every company has to do it. A teaching moment is worth a thousand CEO speeches. CEOs can talk and blab each day about culture, but the employees all know who the jerks are. They could name the jerks for you. It's just cultural. People just don't want to do it."

- Jack Welch (The former CEO of GE who once grew the company by 4,000% during his tenure.)

ASK YOURSELF:

» In what ways can your company begin to implement the use of a stick (penalty) when people fail to deliver on their known expectations?

_____

_____

_____

» In what ways can your company begin to reward the performance of your A-players?

_____

_____

_____

CHAPTER 51

DRAGON ENERGY POWER PRINCIPLE 51

OUTWORK EVERYBODY

THE ENTREPRENEUR'S DRAGON ENERGY

NOTABLE QUOTABLE

"My work ethic came from my father. I don't know anybody who works harder than I do. I'm working all the time. It's not about the money—I just don't know a different way of life, and I love it."

- President Donald J. Trump

President Trump's work ethic is legendary and is frankly something that I pride myself on replicating to an extent. As a happily married man and father of five kids, my number one life goal is to please God, then it's to love my wife the way that Christ loved the church. Thus, I have had to learn to set boundaries in my life for the number of hours I allow myself to work.

Having personally coached hundreds of business owners and having employed countless employees, I can ensure that you the vast majority of Americans are not workaholics. The vast majority of Americans are in fact, sleep-aholics, TV-aholics, gossip-aholics, social-media-aholics, and time-wasting-aholics. So if you do sincerely find yourself in a place where you are really outworking everybody around you and it is becoming a detriment to your family, then consider yourself lucky and make the necessary changes.

NOTABLE QUOTABLE

"I never viewed myself as particularly talented. Where I excel is ridiculous, sickening, work ethic. You know, while the other guy's sleeping, I'm working."

- Will Smith (The American rapper and actor who has been nominated for five Golden Globe Awards and two Academy Awards. Throughout his career he has won four Grammy Awards.)

NOTABLE QUOTABLE

"Work like hell. I mean you just have to put in 80 to 100 hour weeks every week. [This] improves the odds of success. If other people are putting in 40 hour work weeks and you're putting in 100 hour work weeks, then even if you're doing the same thing you know that you will achieve in four months what it takes them a year to achieve."

- Elon Musk

ASK YOURSELF:

» Grade your personal work ethic on a scale of 1 to 10 with 10 being the highest.

_____

» In what ways can you improve the level of diligence and focus that you bring to the workplace on a daily basis?

_____

_____

_____

» How many work days per year do you typically miss because of an excuse that most of the world believes to be valid?

_____

_____

_____

FUN FACT:

If you take off for your birthday, your spouse's birthday, your anniversary, the days before and after each national holiday, two weeks for vacation, and days when you don't feel good while starting or growing a business (before you make your millions), you will be poor.

CIRCLE THE DAYS YOU TOOK OFF THIS PAST YEAR FROM SOWING SEEDS, AND DETERMINE HOW REALISTIC IT IS FOR YOU TO PLAN ON REAPING A HARVEST THIS YEAR.

- The day before New Year's Eve
- New Year's Eve
- New Year's Day
- The day after New Year's Day
- The day before Martin Luther King Jr. Day
- Martin Luther King Jr. Day
- The day after Martin Luther King Jr. Day
- The day before President's Day
- President's Day
- The day after President's Day
- The Thursday before Good Friday
- Good Friday
- The Saturday before Easter
- Easter
- The day after Easter
- The day before Memorial Day
- Memorial Day
- The day after Memorial Day
- The day before Independence Day
- Independence Day
- The day after Independence Day

- The day before Labor Day
- Labor Day
- The day after Labor Day
- The day before Columbus Day
- Columbus Day
- The day after Columbus Day
- The day before Veterans' Day
- Veterans' Day
- The day after Veterans' Day
- The Monday of the week of Thanksgiving
- The Tuesday of the week of Thanksgiving
- The Wednesday of the week of Thanksgiving
- Thanksgiving
- Black Friday
- The day before Christmas Eve (also known as Festivus for all of you Seinfeld fans)
- Christmas Eve
- Christmas Day
- The day after Christmas
- 7 days that you don't feel like coming in because you feel sick
- 104 weekend days off

» In what ways are you wasting time on a daily basis?

_____

_____

_____

If you are running out of time to complete the things that need to be done, then I would encourage you to consider getting rid of your television. The average American now wastes over five hours per day watching TV, according to studies conducted by Nielsen.

If you are sincerely struggling with finding the time to turn your dreams into reality, what ways can you adjust your schedule to create more free time to get things done? If you are struggling to find the time need to get things done, then I would encourage you to discover the incredible hidden pockets of time that you can find between 3a.m. and 7a.m. every day.

NOTABLE QUOTABLE

"When you're around enormously successful people, you realize their success isn't an accident - it's about work."

- Ryan Tedder

THE ENTREPRENEUR'S DRAGON ENERGY

My friend, if you get nothing else out of this book, I would encourage you to develop the habit of always delivering 20% more than you are expected to deliver in every business job that you have. When you choose to consistently show up 20% earlier than you are expected and choose to not "clock in," it wows every boss in America. When you complete your projects 20% ahead of your promised deadlines, you will wow every client in America.

However, if you decide to merely deliver what you promised on time to your ideal and likely buyers, nothing spectacular will happen. You will struggle for your entire career to generate enough word of mouth and referral business to become super profitable. My friend, over time you will see that "When will it be done?" is the question that losers hate to answer and winners who possess "Dragon Energy" love to answer.

NOTABLE QUOTABLE

"Whatever you do, do it well. Do it so well that when people see you do it, they will want to come back and see you do it again, and they will want to bring others and show them how well you do what you do."

- *Walt Disney*

ASK YOURSELF:

» In what ways can you take your work ethic to the next level this year?

_____

_____

_____

» From your perspective, do you consistently overdeliver to your ideal and likely buyers and why?

_____

_____

_____

» In what ways can your business use checklists and documented processes to exceed the expectations of your clients by 20%?

_____

_____

_____

CHAPTER 52

DRAGON ENERGY
POWER PRINCIPLE 52

YOU ARE NOT ALONE (BUT YOU SHOULD BE FOR AT LEAST ONE HOUR PER DAY)

THE ENTREPRENEUR'S DRAGON ENERGY

NOTABLE QUOTABLE

"Got treasures in my mind but couldn't open up my own vault. My childlike creativity, purity and honesty Is honestly being crowded by these grown thoughts."

- Kanye West (From his hit song "POWER")

Whether you are the executive vice president of Walt Disney World Resorts, managing 40,000 employees, or you are a small startup and your job is to just manage yourself, you must stand on top of your responsibilities and be proactive about planning your day. Planning your day is not a group activity. Every single day, you must carve out time into your schedule to set your goals in the areas of:

Faith | *Family* | *Finances* | *Fitness* | *Friendship* | *Fun*

The will to win means nothing without the will to prepare, grind and to get up before 5a.m. every day until you achieve success. If you are not willing to invest your life savings to turn your dreams into reality, then the will to win means nothing. You have to be willing to do the things that you don't want to do but have to do in order to turn your dreams into reality. When you have the self-discipline required to spend at least one hour alone per day, you will find yourself more prepared for the work day, more proactive as a human, and more purposeful and intentional about every aspect of your life. If you aren't used to spending time alone and preparing your day proactively, answer the following questions and you will be off to a great start:

ASK YOURSELF:

» What is the best time of the day for you to plan your day?

_____

_____

_____

» Where is the best place for you to plan your day?

_____

_____

_____

» What do you need to have with you to have a productive planning session (background music, dry erase board, computer, journal, etc)?

_____

_____

_____

CHAPTER 53

DRAGON ENERGY POWER PRINCIPLE 53

LEARN TO F.O.C.U.S.

THE ENTREPRENEUR'S DRAGON ENERGY

NOTABLE QUOTABLE

"I like to think of the word FOCUS as Follow
One Course Until Successful."

- President Donald J. Trump

My brother-in-law and I first had the vision to franchise Elephant In The Room Men's Grooming Lounge seven years before we opened our first franchise. I started recording podcasts nearly two years before I released our first podcast. Babies are conceived nine months before they ever see the light of day. Seeds, if properly planted in an environment that provides consistent 60 degree to 95 degree temperature, take between 60 and 100 days to grow. I realize that we now live in a microwave society filled with Instagram and the desire for instant fame, instant results, and instant success, but that is just not how the world of entrepreneurship works.

My friend, the path to your success is about saying no to everything that is a distraction to you and the achievement of your goals. You don't have to live a life filled with obligations and invitations to events that will be filled with surface-level conversations and people who you barely know. You don't have to wish everyone you know a happy birthday on Facebook. You don't have to go to your high school reunion. You must decide today that you will control your destiny, or somebody else certainly will. If success was determined by great ideas then everyone would be rich. My friend, it's about execution and results not ideas and hope.

NOTABLE QUOTABLE

"People think focus means saying yes to the thing
you've got to focus on. But that's not what it means at
all. It means saying no to the hundred other good ideas
that there are. You have to pick carefully. I'm actually
as proud of the things we haven't done as the things I
have done. Innovation is saying no to 1,000 things."

- Steve Jobs

ASK YOURSELF:

» What do you need to start saying no to?

_____

_____

_____

» Where was your time spent yesterday? (Take the time to write it all out)

_____

_____

_____

» In what ways are you chasing the addiction of new ideas instead of committing and focusing on your big idea?

_____

_____

_____

» How much time did you spend watching TV this week?

_____

_____

_____

» How much time did you spend being perpetually distracted by your smartphone?

_____

_____

_____

THE ENTREPRENEUR'S DRAGON ENERGY

FUN FACT:

"Here's another disturbing stat: This tally seems to increase daily, but by one study's count, the typical smartphone user interacts with their phone around 85 times per day. And this often includes middle-of-the-night checks for work emails and new 'likes.'"

—Anna Akbari Ph.D. - "Why Your Smartphone is Destroying Your Life" - https://www.psychologytoday. com/us/blog/startup-your-life/201801/why-your-smartphone-is-destroying-your-life

FUN FACT:

"According to Nielsen reports, the average American watches 5 hours of TV per day."

- https://www.nydailynews.com/life-style/average-american-watches-5-hours-tv-day-article-1.1711954

CHAPTER 54

DRAGON ENERGY POWER PRINCIPLE 54

BUY ASSETS, NOT LIABILITIES

THE ENTREPRENEUR'S DRAGON ENERGY

People without "Dragon Energy" are stuck in the cycle of buying material things they can barely afford to impress neighbors, co-workers, and people on social media that they barely know. People with "Dragon Energy" live below their means and focus exclusively on buying things that will make them more money. Simply put, assets are things that put additional money and income into your pocket. Liabilities are things that take money out of your pocket. To help you cut through the clutter, I've put together a list of example assets and a list of example liabilities:

ASSETS:

- » Rental homes that produce you positive cash flow
- » Trademarks
- » Patents
- » Copyrights
- » Franchises
- » Licensing agreements
- » New skills that people are willing to pay for
- » Stocks
- » Bonds
- » Products
- » Real estate
- » Businesses
- » Machinery and equipment used to generate a profit
- » Anything that adds money into your pocket.

LIABILITIES:

- » A car
- » The home you live in should be considered as an asset the vast majority of the time, but most Americans do not typically make money as a result of owning it (but you could).
- » Subscriptions to magazines you don't read
- » Timeshares
- » Credit card debt
- » Consumer debt accumulated by buying furniture, flat screens,

and fancy refrigerators with the newest smart gadget technology.

» Anything that takes money out of your pocket.

NOTABLE QUOTABLE

"You must know the difference between an asset and a liability, and buy assets.... Rich people acquire assets. Poor and middle class people acquire liabilities, but they think they are assets."

- Robert Kiyosaki (The best-selling co-author of the Rich Dad Poor Dad book series.)

ASK YOURSELF:

» What liabilities have you bought in the past year?

_____

_____

_____

» What assets have you purchased in the past year?

_____

_____

_____

» What is the difference between an asset and a liability?

_____

_____

_____

CHAPTER 55

DRAGON ENERGY POWER PRINCIPLE 55

UNDERSTAND THAT MASSIVE PAY COMES WITH MASSIVE RESPONSIBILITY

THE ENTREPRENEUR'S DRAGON ENERGY

At our business conferences, many wonderful people share with me that they want to "get where I am now." I explain to them that they absolutely must have the mental capacity to make it happen; however, I challenge them about whether they truly want to "get where I am now" because of the responsibility that comes with what I do. I release podcasts per week, and that's even on the days that I don't feel like it. I am constantly dealing with intense adversity from people that we've had to fire, competitors who are hell-bent on destroying us by any means necessary, and the endless friction that is created when you have to say "no" to virtually everything all of the time. I personally love living behind the wall at Camp Clark and Chicken Palace. I enjoy the pool, I enjoy reading books in a literal cave behind the waterfall, and I enjoy both the time and financial freedom that I have, but this time and financial freedom has come at a great price—a price that I was willing to pay.

ASK YOURSELF:

» What are you willing to trade off to get what you want?

_____

_____

» Are you willing to trade off watching five hours of TV (like the average American now does) to achieve your goals?

_____

_____

» Are you willing to trade off engaging with social media to achieve your goals?

_____

_____

» Are you willing to trade off interacting with toxic family members to achieve your goals (this involves punting them out of your life)?

_____

_____

» Are you willing to stop involving yourself in organizations that are not helping you to get closer to the achievement of your goals?

_____

_____

» What are you willing to give up in exchange for the life you want to live and the goals you are looking to achieve?

_____

_____

CHAPTER 56

DRAGON ENERGY POWER PRINCIPLE 56

REFUSE TO SPEND TIME WITH PEOPLE CONTENT WITH LOSING

THE ENTREPRENEUR'S DRAGON ENERGY

NOTABLE QUOTABLE

"I don't like losers."

- President Donald J. Trump

Unfortunately, losing is contagious. It gets complicated because people who perpetually lose don't want to be labeled as losers, so they start to lower their standards and say stupid things like, "to me it's really not about winning; it's about having fun playing the game." My friend, you would never hear these comments from Michael Jordan, Kobe Bryant, Tom Brady, or anybody who has ever played a game or dominated an industry at a high level.

NOTABLE QUOTABLE

"I'm addicted to winning. The more you win, the more you want to win."

- Larry Ellison (The co-founder of the Oracle Corporation. As of 2018, he was listed by Forbes as being the 5th wealthiest person in America with a fortune of $54.5 billion)

NOTABLE QUOTABLE

"I think that at the start of a game, you're always playing to win, and then maybe if you're ahead late in the game, you start playing not to lose. The true competitors, though, are the ones who always play to win."

- Tom Brady

As you read this, I would encourage you to consider whether you are hanging around with winners or whiners? Are you hanging out with people who set high standards for themselves and for others, or are you hanging out with people that have a losing, socialistic, casual attitude?

NOTABLE QUOTABLE

"The passive ironic attitude is not cool or romantic, but pathetic and destructive."

- Robert Greene

Is it ok with you if I get REAL and REALLY INTENSE with you for just a second? Okay, so this is how life works: every person involved in your life is either a negative or a positive, and that includes you, your employees, your spouse, your cousins, your extended family, your acquaintances, your Facebook friends - everybody that you are connected to in some way. So you must be intense about not allowing negative people, high-drama people, constant full-page emailers, social media agitators, and people with huge life issues into your life on a consistent basis. Otherwise, your light will be extinguished by their jackassery, their negativity, and their constant drama.

NOTABLE QUOTABLE

"Walk with the wise and become wise, for a companion of fools suffers harm."

- Proverbs 13:20

ASK YOURSELF:

» Are you currently a perpetual loser and if so, why?

_____

_____

_____

» Who in your life is a perpetual loser?

_____

_____

_____

» Who in your life constantly emails or texts you negative things?

_____

_____

_____

» Who should you begin to spend more time with?

_____

_____

_____

» Who should you begin to spend less time with?

_____

_____

_____

CHAPTER 57

DRAGON ENERGY
POWER PRINCIPLE **57**

SHUT UP AND CREATE A REAL PRODUCT OR SERVICE

NOTABLE QUOTABLE

"You must have a real product or service that solves real problems for real ideal and likely buyers or you don't have a real business."

- Clay Clark

So often, throughout my speaking career, I've met people who have refused to embrace the "Dragon Energy" and therefore they run around acting like their ideas matter more than the results. For example, years ago, we had a man reach out to us who had this vision to "DRAMATICALLY ALTER THE REAL ESTATE INDUSTRY" forever by charging a flat low rate to sell homes. Currently, in the world of real estate, somehow 6% has become the commission rate that the modern American world has concluded is a fair amount of commission to pay to the real estate agents involved in helping you market and sell your home.

That means if you are selling a $100,000 piece of real estate, $6,000 in commission would be paid out at the time of closing. If you are selling a $600,000 piece of real estate, $36,000 would be paid out in real estate commission at the time of closing. I think we can all see the problem here. It doesn't make sense to pay someone $36,000 in commission to sell a $600,000 house, but somehow in the world of real estate professionals, this makes sense to all of the real estate agents in America, while making zero sense to the average consumer.

So, a man reached out to me and told me that he had this plan to "change the game in the world of real estate" by charging a flat fee of $1,000 to anybody looking to sell their home.

The idea sounded great. We all felt great about the idea. But none of that mattered unless he was actually willing to put in the work to market the crap out of this idea. He also had to accept the face that he would have to fight with all of the real estate agents in his local city who would think that "flat rate" real estate was unethical.

As it turned out, he was not willing to put in the work to educate his local community, and he did not have the work ethic needed to turn his idea into reality. That would have required waking up at 4:0a.m. or 5:00a.m. and actually making things happen. He wasn't willing to invest the thousands of dollars per week needed to market the business and the concept to his community via Google, Facebook, Youtube, and every other online digital marketing platform at our disposal. Actually, he wasn't willing to do anything, yet he expressed to me directly on multiple occasions that he felt that other real estate companies needed to pay him because they were using his idea without his permission. As it turned out, despite his desire for the world to operate differently, our legal system currently does not reward people for having ideas that have not been patented, copyrighted, or trademarked because JUST HAVING A FREAKING IDEA DOES NOT MATTER.

On the planet Earth, in a capitalist society, bottom line, we only get paid for the results that we deliver and no one gives a crap about our ideas. My friend, if ideas did matter, then every pothead I've met at a local Denver coffee shop would be the millionaires and billionaires leading the free world. All of those smoked out granolas with "anxiety problems" have endless ideas to "end world hunger" to "make the planet more sustainable" and to "stop of the problems caused by inequality."

NOTABLE QUOTABLE

"Vision without execution is hallucination."

- Thomas Edison

THE ENTREPRENEUR'S DRAGON ENERGY

ASK YOURSELF:

» In what ways have you been trying to get the world to pay you for your ideas and not your results?

_____

_____

_____

» What do you need to do to turn your ideas into reality?

_____

_____

_____

» Have you ever tried to market a bogus product or service in the hopes of getting rich quick?

_____

_____

_____

NOTE: If you have ever gotten caught up in trying to get rich quick, don't feel

bad; just stop trying to do it. In fact, the desire to get something for nothing

has been around for thousands of years.

NOTABLE QUOTABLE

"Wealth from get-rich-quick schemes quickly disappears; wealth from hard work grows over time. Hope deferred makes the heart sick, but a dream fulfilled is a tree of life. People who despise advice are asking for trouble; those who respect a command will succeed."

- Proverbs 13:11–13

CHAPTER 58

DRAGON ENERGY
POWER PRINCIPLE 58

BELIEVE YOU CAN ACHIEVE YOUR GOALS

THE ENTREPRENEUR'S DRAGON ENERGY

I don't know if you are battling internal demons that are telling you that you can't succeed or that you don't have what it takes, but if you are, understand this: I had to take Algebra three times just to pass, and I also had to take my ACT three times just to get into college. I am a prime example of someone who has been able to achieve success without being super smart or super educated. In fact, most of the world's industries have been created by people who did not do well in formal schooling, or who did not have the perceived prerequisite pedigree for professional prominence that people believe they must have to succeed.

The following entrepreneurs and world leaders struggled through life because they didn't have a degree from a fancy business college (forgive the sarcasm spasms):

ABRAHAM LINCOLN

Despite not having earned the respect of his peers by obtaining a college degree, he went on to become a lawyer and president of the United States. Because he chose to be self-taught, he never stopped learning until the day of his death.

» 1832 - Lost his job and was defeated for state legislature.

» 1833 - Failed in business.

» 1843 - Lost his attempt to be nominated for Congress.

» 1848 - Lost renomination for Congress.

» 1849 - Rejected in his attempt to become land officer.

- » 1854 - Defeated for U.S. Senate.

- » 1856 - Defeated for nomination for vice president.

- » 1848 - Defeated for U.S. Senate.

- » 1860 - November 6th 1860 Abraham Lincoln was elected the 16th President of the United States.

AMADEO PETER GIANNINI

Despite not knowing what he was doing because he didn't have a master's degree from a fancy business college, he went on to become the multi-millionaire founder of Bank of America after dropping out of high school.

ANDREW CARNEGIE

Despite being an elementary school dropout, this man went on to become the world's wealthiest man during his lifetime. Amazing, since he couldn't possibly have known what he was doing because he didn't have a college degree.

ANDREW JACKSON

This guy went on to become an attorney, a U.S. president, a general, a judge, and a congressman despite being home-schooled and having no formal education at all.

ANNE BEILER

The "Princess of Pretzels" went on to start Auntie Anne's Pretzels and became a millionaire, despite having dropped out of high school.

I bet she's disappointed she missed out on the once-in-a-lifetime experiences that so many college graduates with $100,000 of debt enjoyed.

ANSEL ADAMS

I don't know if you are into world-famous photographers or not, but if you are, you know that Ansel Adams became arguably the best photographer in the world despite not graduating from a college of liberal arts. I wonder how he even knew to take the lens cap off of his camera without a college degree.

BARRY DILLER

This dude may be a billionaire and Hollywood mogul who founded Fox Broadcasting Company, but I am not impressed with him because he does not have a college degree.

BENJAMIN FRANKLIN

This guy might have invented the Franklin stove, lightning rods, bifocals, and other assorted inventions while working as a founding father of the United States, but I can tell you that he had a hole in his soul where his degree should have been.

BILLY JOE (RED) McCOMBS

Red became a billionaire, but did he have a degree? No. And that is exactly why he doesn't get invited to any of those fancy alumni gatherings, which he would be too busy to attend anyway because he's off counting his money. Seriously, if he started counting the billions of dollars he made by founding Clear Channel media, he would never finish.

BILL GATES

He started that little company that Steve Jobs fought. That's it. As the owner of Microsoft, he can take his $53 billion and go buy boats, houses, and stuff, but he can't buy the memories that he missed out on by not graduating from college.

COCO CHANEL

She may have a perfume that bears her name, but I am not impressed with her because she doesn't have a degree.

COLONEL HARLAN SANDERS

This guy, the founder of KFC, dropped out of elementary school and all he knew about was chicken. Sure, he made millions, but I didn't truly have respect for him until he finally earned that law degree by correspondence.

DAVE THOMAS

Every time I pull into Wendy's to enjoy a delicious snack wrap, I find myself thinking about what a complete waste of talent Dave was. He could have had trillions of dollars if only he had earned a degree.

DAVID GEFFEN

Like a true loser, he dropped out of college after completing only one year. My, his parents must be disappointed. I feel bad just writing about this billionaire founder of Geffen Records and co-founder of DreamWorks.

DAVID GREEN

David, oh David. I bet you feel bad about your billions and spend every day living in regret because you do not have a college degree. I know that you took $600 and famously turned that into billions as the founder of Hobby Lobby, but you could have been a good attorney, or a bureaucrat, or a politician we all could have watched argue to an empty room on C-SPAN.

DAVID KARP

This guy's last name should be carp, because this bottom feeder obviously will never amount to anything – well, except being the multi-millionaire founder of Tumblr. If he hadn't dropped out of school at age 15, I would respect him more.

DAVID NEELEMAN

This guy started a little airline (JetBlue) to compensate for his lack of a degree. I don't even feel safe on the world's most profitable airline because its founder doesn't have a degree.

DAVID ORECK

David Oreck truly had a career that sucked. This college dropout and multi-millionaire founder of the Oreck vacuum company created vacuums that have sucked the dirt out of carpets for years.

DEBBI FIELDS

Oh, so sad. Little Debbie, the founder Mrs. Fields Chocolate Chippery, never knew the pride that one could feel upon earning a college degree.

DEWITT WALLACE

DeWitt may have founded Reader's Digest, but I'm sure that he could not truly enjoy reading in an intelligent way because he never earned his college degree.

DUSTIN MOSKOVITZ

Dustin is credited as being one of the founders of that little company called Facebook that only moms, dads, cousins, kids, adults, and humans use. I bet he wishes he had stayed in school at Harvard.

FRANK LLOYD WRIGHT

Frank may have become the most famous architect of all time, but I cannot respect a man who had never attended high school.

FREDERICK HENRY ROYCE

Okay, so a Rolls-Royce is a symbol of automotive excellence for many people, but this guy had to have been compensating for the fact that he knew nothing about anything because he was an elementary school dropout.

GEORGE EASTMAN

Perhaps you are not old enough to know about the Kodak brand that used to control the world of photography. However, George founded this little company despite dropping out of high school is beyond me. It's so sad.

THE ENTREPRENEUR'S DRAGON ENERGY

HENRY FORD

Okay, so I've mentioned this guy in the book, but without a college degree, you can bet this billionaire founder of the Ford Motor Company was never respected by his father-in-law.

HENRY J. KAISER

This multimillionaire and founder of Kaiser Aluminum didn't even graduate from high school. Think about it. Without a diploma, there was no way he could have become one of those pharmaceutical reps who deliver sales presentations and cater to doctors every day in exchange for their allegiance in writing prescriptions for the drugs the rep is peddling.

HYMAN GOLDEN

This guy spent his whole life making drinks and millions. I bet you the founder of Snapple lived a life of regret while endlessly chanting to himself, "Why me? No Degree. Why me? No degree."

INGVAR KAMPRAD

I believe IKEA's business model is in jeopardy. Their founder has no degree. The lines of customers are now so long that no one even wants to go there anymore. Oh . . . and he's dyslexic.

ISAAC MERRIT SINGER

This sewing machine inventor dropped out of high school because he was spending all his time sewing. I am SEW sorry for him.

JACK CRAWFORD TAYLOR

Although this man did serve honorably as a World War II fighter pilot for the Navy, I wonder what he is going to fall back on if his Enterprise Rent-a-Car venture fails.

JAMES CAMERON

Avatar . . . overrated. Titanic . . . overrated. Winning an Oscar . . . overrated. But what did you expect from a director, writer, and film guy who dropped out of college?

JAY VAN ANDEL

A billionaire co-founder of Amway . . . not impressive without a degree. He does not know the meaning of life.

JAY-Z

Despite not having a college degree Jay-z has become one of the most well known an successful artists and entrepreneurs in America. Throughout his music career he has earned 22 Grammy Awards, and throughout his business career he has been able to build a networth of $900 million according to Forbes as a result of his successful business ventures and investments with Rocaware clothing line, Roc-A-Fella Records, the 40/40 Club sports bar, Def Jam Recordings, the Brooklyn Nets, Armand de Brignac champagne, the Roc Nation Sports agency and the Barclays Center.

THE ENTREPRENEUR'S DRAGON ENERGY

 JERRY YANG

Who even uses Yahoo! anyway, other than the 20% of the world that does? This guy threw it all away and dropped out of a PhD program. I bet you he can't even spell "Yahoo!"

 JIMMY DEAN

Food is so simple. You grow it. You eat it. You raise it. You kill it and eat it. How complex could it be if a man was able to start this multi-million dollar company after dropping out of high school at age 16?

 JIMMY LOVINE

This man grew up as the son of a secretary and a longshoreman. However, at the age of 19, his ambition had become his mission. Obsessed with making records, he began working as a studio professional around the year of 1972 when a friend of his landed him a job cleaning a recording studio. Soon, he found himself recording with John Lennon, Bruce Springsteen and other top artists. In 1973, he landed a full-time job on the staff of the New York recording studio, Record Plant, where he worked on Meat Loaf's Bat Out of Hell album and Springsteen's Born to Run album. He went on to be involved in the production of more than 250 million albums.

In 2006, Lovine teamed with Dr. Dre to found Beats Electronics. This company was purchased by Apple for $3 billion in May 2014. I hope he goes on to be successful despite not having a degree.

JOEL OSTEEN

Despite not having a college degree from a divinity school, Joel Osteen was able to successfully take over for his father John Osteen as the senior Pastor of Lakewood Church. Since October 3rd, 1999, Joel and his wife Victoria have grown the church from 5,000 to 43,000 weekly attendees, and he has written seven books which have been on the New York Times Best Seller list. In order to accommodate the growing attendance of this congregation, Joel successfully negotiated the purchase of the former home of the NBA Houston Rockets that was formerly known as the Compaq Center. After purchasing the building, the Lakewood Church invested $105 million to transform the aging basketball arena into a modern church. Lakewood's 2005 grand opening was attended by 56,000 people.

JOHN D. ROCKEFELLER SR.

So my son and I did name our Great Pyrenees dog after this man, but we wouldn't have named a human after him, because although Rockefeller became the wealthiest man in the world, he didn't have a degree and I judge him for this.

JOHN MACKEY

The guy who founded Whole Foods Market, the millennial mecca of the great organic panic that has swept our nation, enrolled and dropped out of college six times. Now he's stuck working at a grocery store in a dead-end job.

JOHN PAUL DEJORIA

This man is the billionaire co-founder of John Paul Mitchell Systems, and is the dude who also founded Patron Spirits. That's it. That's all he's accomplished. No degree.

THE ENTREPRENEUR'S DRAGON ENERGY

JOYCE C. HALL

This guy spent his whole life writing apology cards to his family for shaming them by not graduating from college. When he wasn't doing that, he was running that little company he founded called Hallmark.

KEMMONS WILSON

This dude started the Holiday Inn chain after dropping out of high school. But then what? What's he doing now? Well, he's not buying huge amounts of college logo apparel and running down to the college football stadium eight Saturdays per year while talking about the good old days with his frat brothers because he doesn't have a degree.

KEVIN ROSE

This dude dropped out of college and started a company called Digg.com. I'm not impressed with his millions. I just want to see that degree.

KIRK KERKORIAN

I did see a Boyz II Men concert at the Mirage Resorts that this guy owns. But, I have never stayed at the Mandalay Bay resort that he owns in Las Vegas more than once. It's good that he owns MGM Studios, because the closest he'll ever come to a degree is if he makes a movie about himself getting a degree. He dropped out of school in 8th grade.

LARRY ELLISON

Larry is the billionaire co-founder of Oracle software company, and he dropped out of two different colleges. Oh, the regret he must feel.

LEANDRO RIZZUTO

This guy spent his time building Conair and that was it. Now, just because he is billionaire, does he think we should respect him even though he does not have a degree?

LESLIE WEXNER

My wife buys stuff from the L Brands (the global retail empire that owns Victoria's Secret, Bath & Body Works, and The Limited), but I am still not impressed with the fact that this law school dropout started a billion-dollar brand with $5,000.

MARK ECKO

If you are one of those people who is impressed by real self-made success, then I suppose Mark Ecko is impressive. This multi-millionaire is the founder of Mark Ecko Enterprises, but he dropped out of college.

MARY KAY ASH

I feel like Prince should have written a song about the pink Cadillacs that Mary Kay was famous for giving to her top sales reps. But I am not impressed with her because she didn't attend college.

MICHAEL DELL

He may be the billionaire founder of Dell Computers, but he probably doesn't feel like a billionaire since he never experienced the college joys of drunken music festivals and regrettable one-night stands.

MILTON HERSHEY

Like I always say, "If you drop out of 4th grade, you are going to spend your entire life making chocolate." That is what the founder of Hershey's Milk Chocolate did.

 RACHAEL RAY

Her happiness and genuine love for people and food makes me mad because without formal culinary arts training, this Food Network cooking show star and food industry entrepreneur is just a sham.

 RAY KROC

He dropped out of high school, founded McDonald's, and spent his whole life asking, "Do you want fries with that?" So sad.

 RICHARD BRANSON

So he's the billionaire founder of Virgin Records, Virgin Atlantic Airways, Virgin Mobile and more. But did he graduate from high school? No. He dropped out of high school at the age of 16. So sad.

 RICHARD SCHULZE

He's the founder of Best Buy, but he did not attend college. Doesn't he know that the investment in a college degree is truly the Best Buy you can ever make?

ROB KALIN

Rob is the founder of Etsy, but who even uses Etsy other than all of the humans on earth? This dude flunked out of high school, then he enrolled in art school. He created a fake student ID for MIT so he could take the courses that he wanted. His professors were so impressed by his scam that they actually helped him get into NYU. Rob, you have to get it together.

RON POPEIL

The dude who is constantly talking about dehydrating your meat, and the multimillionaire founder of Ronco did not graduate from college.

RUSH LIMBAUGH

This guy irritates half of America every day for three hours per day. I believe that this multi-millionaire media maven and radio talk show host would be more liked if he had graduated from a liberal arts college and purchased a Prius pre-loaded with left-wing bumper stickers.

RUSSELL SIMMONS

This guy is co-founder of Def Jam Recordings and the founder of the Russell Simmons Music Group. He's also the founder of Phat Farm fashions and is a best-selling author. He didn't graduate from college because he claims to have been too busy introducing rap and hip hop music to the planet.

S. DANIEL ABRAHAM

This man founded Slim-Fast without even having a degree in nutrition. Outside of the millions of people who use his products every day to lose weight, who is going to trust him with their health since he doesn't even have a college degree?

THE ENTREPRENEUR'S DRAGON ENERGY

SEAN JOHN COMBS

The man who is en route to becoming the first hip hop billionaire in part because of his ownership in the Ciroc Vodka brand did not graduate from college because he was spending his time discovering and promoting Mary J. Blige, The Notorious B.I.G., Jodeci and other R&B stars. If this man ever wants to become truly successful, he will go back to Howard University and get that degree.

SHAWN FANNING

This is the music industry-killing devil who created Napster and went on to become a multi-millionaire. If he would have stayed in college, he would have learned to follow the rules.

SIMON COWELL

This famous TV producer, judger of people and star of American Idol, The X Factor, and Britain's Got Talent dropped out of high school. He has been negative ever since. He obviously needs a college degree to calm him down because I've never met a college graduate who is mean.

STEVE JOBS

This hippie dropped out of college and frankly, his little Apple company barely made it.

STEVE MADDEN

Steve dropped out of college and now spends his entire life making shoes. He may be worth millions, but I'm sure that you are not impressed.

STEVE WOZNIAK

Okay, so I did know that Steve Jobs co-founded Apple with this guy and both of them became billionaires, but they experienced what I call "hollow success" because they did not take the time to earn a college degree.

THEODORE WAITT

This man became a billionaire by selling a PC to every human possible during the 1990s. He may have co-founded Gateway computers but without a degree, how will he ever experience true success? I bet he regrets not having a degree.

THOMAS EDISON

Tommy Boy wasn't smart enough to graduate from high school, yet he was crazy enough to invent the modern light bulb, recorded audio and recorded video. I am never impressed with crazy people who don't graduate from high school.

TOM ANDERSON

This man co-founded MySpace after dropping out of high school. He made his millions, but who ever had a MySpace account anyway?

THE ENTREPRENEUR'S DRAGON ENERGY

TY WARNER

I think the only thing weirder than collecting Beanie Babies is to have invented them. To cover up this weird Beanie Babies fixation, this billionaire has gone on to purchase real estate. College would have taught him that it is not normal for an adult to be interested in stuffed animals.

W. CLEMENT STONE

This guy started the billion-dollar insurance company called Combined Insurance. He then went on to start Success magazine and wrote books to keep himself busy because he felt so bad that he didn't have a college degree.

WALLY "FAMOUS" AMOS

This man did not graduate from high school, and spent almost his entire working career making people fat by selling them Famous Amos cookies. If he had graduated from college, he might have invented a product that makes people thin and able to live forever while tasting good, you know, like carrots.

WALT DISNEY

This struggling entrepreneur who never really figured it out co-founded the Walt Disney Company with his brother Roy. He didn't even graduate from high school, which is probably why he spent his entire life drawing cartoons.

WOLFGANG PUCK

Okay, so my wife and I buy his soup. Okay, so I have eaten at his restaurant a few times.

But I can't respect a man who dropped out of high school at the age of 14. Yes, he's opened up 16 restaurants and 80 bistros. So what? Respecting people like this sets a bad example for kids because not everyone can go on to become a successful entrepreneur, but everyone can incur $100,000 of student loan debt before finding a soul-sucking job doing something they don't like in exchange for a paycheck.

ASK YOURSELF:

> » what negative psycho-babble and self-talk have you been filling your brain with that has caused you to believe that you don't have what it takes to succeed?

_____

_____

_____

Decide here and now that you believe that you have what it takes to succeed in the game of life and business by signing your name to the following statement of faith: I believe that I have what it takes to achieve success, and I will not allow myself to fill my mind with negativity and self-doubt ever again.

> » First and Last Name:

_____

> » Signature:

_____

> » Date:

_____

CHAPTER 59

DRAGON ENERGY POWER PRINCIPLE 59

DON'T WORRY ABOUT EVERYBODY ELSE; FOCUS ON BECOMING THE BEST YOU CAN BE

NOTABLE QUOTABLE

"Criticism is easier to take when you realize
that the only people who aren't criticized
are those who don't take risks."

—*President Donald J. Trump*

As an entrepreneur, I am used to getting non-actionable and non-practical feedback from everybody who has the mental capacity to send an email or make a phone call. Although the vast majority of feedback that I receive from people unhelpful, I have received many powerful, practical and actionable bits of advice and feedback from our ideal and likely buyers over the years. Thus, my advice to you is this: gather feedback from your ideal and likely buyers, and don't worry if the criticism is harsh because it's probably helpful. Whenever somebody is spending both their time and their money with your organization, their expectations will elevate. However, don't spend your time as an entrepreneur gathering feedback from people who are not your ideal and likely buyers because they don't get it, they don't want it, and everybody has an opinion.

NOTABLE QUOTABLE

"Listening to uninformed people is worse
than having no answers at all."

—*Ray Dalio*

NOTABLE QUOTABLE

"Your most unhappy customers are your
greatest source of learning."

—*Bill Gates*

ASK YOURSELF:

» Whose feedback do you need to stop listening to?

_____

_____

_____

» Whose feedback do you need to start valuing more?

_____

_____

_____

» Whose feedback do you need to begin seeking out?

_____

_____

_____

CHAPTER 60

DRAGON ENERGY POWER PRINCIPLE 60

BRING YOUR A-GAME EVERYDAY (ESPECIALLY ON THE DAYS WHEN YOU DON'T FEEL GOOD)

THE ENTREPRENEUR'S DRAGON ENERGY

Many years ago Doctor Zoellner told me, "Every customer experience is show time," and that set me free of the poverty mindset that always said, "I don't want to sell out. I want to keep it real." And my friend, let me break this down for you. People who refuse to "sell out" and bring their A-game everyday at work because they want to be more "authentic" and "transparent" are going to be poor. The people who want to share with the world how they feel at all times because they want to "keep it real" will always be "real poor."

ASK YOURSELF:

» In what ways are you only bringing your best performance on the days that you feel like it?

_____

_____

_____

» How could you improve your daily work performance?

_____

_____

_____

» How many days during the past 90 days have you brought less than your A-game to work?

_____

_____

» What do you need to do in your morning routine to create an internal momentum needed to bring your personal best to the workplace each day (working out, meditating in the morning, reading in the morning before work, etc.)?

_____

_____

_____

CHAPTER 61

DRAGON ENERGY
POWER PRINCIPLE **61**

ACCEPT THAT YOU CAN CREATE MORE MONEY, BUT YOU CAN'T MAKE MORE TIME

THE ENTREPRENEUR'S DRAGON ENERGY

NOTABLE QUOTABLE

"The only luxury is time. The time you get to spend
with your family."

- Kanye West

Throughout my career, I've had the opportunity to interview millionaires, and even billionaires through those conversations discovered that all top performers have a reverence for time that most of the population lacks. Super successful people are fastidious about being on time, respecting people's time, getting things done on time, and refusing to wasting time, YOU SHOULD BE TOO if you want to take your life and business to the next level. Vanessa, my wife of over 18 years, I want to apologize for ever wasting any of OUR time talking to idiots, meeting with idiots, and attempting to reason with idiots.

NOTABLE QUOTABLE

"You either pay now or pay later with just
about every decision you make about
where and how you spend your time."

—Lee Cockerell

NOTABLE QUOTABLE

"The quality of your life is directly affected by
how and where you spend your time."

—Lee Cockerell

NOTABLE QUOTABLE

"Until you value yourself, you will not value your time. Until
you value your time, you will not do anything with it."

—Lee Cockerell

ASK YOURSELF:

» In what ways are you perpetually wasting time?

_____

_____

_____

» In what ways are you wasting other people's time?

_____

_____

_____

» In what ways could you optimize how you are using your time?

_____

_____

_____

» Who do you need to stop investing your time with?

_____

_____

_____

CHAPTER 62

DRAGON ENERGY POWER PRINCIPLE 62

ACCEPT THAT 1,000 NO'S CREATES 1 YES

THE ENTREPRENEUR'S DRAGON ENERGY

Don't overthink this and don't ask me for statistical proof that 1,000 no's will create one yes, but you must accept the truth of what I'm saying. On our Thrivetime Show Podcast, we have interviewed super successful guests from all around the world over the years, only because I get rejected by more people than you can possibly imagine. Most people want to focus on the past guests that we have interviewed including:

» The New York Times best-selling co-author of *Rich Dad Poor Dad*, Sharon Lechter.

» Senior Editor for Forbes and best-selling author of *3 Kings*, *Michael Jackson Inc.*, and *Empire State of Mind: How JAY-Z Went From Street Corner To Corner Office*, Zack O'Malley Greenburg.

» Creator of EOFire.com and the most downloaded business podcaster of all-time, John Lee Dumas.

» The New York Times best-selling author of *Purple Cow* and former Yahoo! Vice President of marketing, Seth Godin.

» Co-Founder of the 700+ employee advertising company AdRoll, Adam Berke.

» Emmy award-winning producer of the Today Show and The New York Times best-selling author of *Sh*tty Moms*, Mary Ann Zoellner.

» The New York Times best-selling author of *Contagious: Why Things Catch On* and Wharton Business School professor, Jonah Berger

» The New York Times best-selling author of *Made to Stick* and Duke University professor, Dan Heath

» International best-selling author of *In Search of Excellence*, Tom Peters

» NBA player and coach, and the shortest player to ever play in the league, Muggsy Bogues

» NFL running back and winner of Dancing with the Stars, Rashad Jennings

» NBA Hall of Famer, two-time NBA Champion, and two-time Olympic Gold Medalist, David Robinson

» The former executive vice president of Walt Disney World who once managed 40,000 employees, Lee Cockerell

» Michael Levine, the PR consultant of choice for Michael Jackson, Prince, Nike, Charlton Heston, Nancy Kerrigan and others

» Johnny G, the inventor of the spin class phenomenon, Spinning®

» Wes Carter, the attorney for TD Jakes and Joyce Meyers

» Paul Pressey, 10-year NBA player, 20+ year NBA assistant coach for the Los Angeles Lakers, the Orlando Magic, the Boston Celtics and others

» Rachel Faucett, the inventor and social media advisor of choice for Disney, Pottery Barn, and Hobby Lobby

» Jill Donovan, "Mom-Preneur" and retail product developer whose products have been worn by Oprah, Britney Spears and countless celebrities

» The best-selling author of *Search Engine for Dummies*, Bruce Clay

» Billboard contemporary chart-topping singer-songwriter and Atlantic Records recording artist, Colton Dixon

» Conservative talk pundit, frequent Fox News contributor, political commentator and best-selling author, Ben Shapiro

However, en route to booking these super successful people, I have been repeatedly rejected by Tim Tebow, coach Bill Parcells, coach Bill Belichick, TD Jakes, and a massive list of other big-time people who simply cannot justify taking time out of their schedule to appear on our podcast. But this does not deter me in the least because I will not stop reaching out until they all cry, buy, or die. I am relentless because I believe in what I do, and I know that 1,000 no's will produce one yes. Did you know that each week, we get rejected by nearly 1,000 potential guests en route to booking our five to seven actual confirmed interviewees and show guests?

NOTABLE QUOTABLE

"Successful people don't fear failure. But understand that it's necessary to learn and grow from."

- Robert Kiyosaki

ASK YOURSELF:

» In what way are you simply not getting rejected enough?

_____

_____

_____

» How many no's do you need to get per yes in your industry?

_____

_____

_____

» How many rejections have you received this month?

_____

_____

_____

» How many rejections do you need to receive next month
in order to reach your goals?

_____

_____

_____

CHAPTER 63

DRAGON ENERGY
POWER PRINCIPLE **63**

MANIACALLY OBSESS ABOUT ONE IDEA FOR A DECADE

THE ENTREPRENEUR'S DRAGON ENERGY

NOTABLE QUOTABLE

"I'm only interested in big ideas that aren't easy to execute. These take a long time to get going, but when they do, you can see the light at the end of the tunnel showing you how they could become big, game-changing businesses, and therefore good investments. More important, they could become transformative forces in terms of improving people's lives."

—*Steve Case*

AMPLE EXAMPLES of Great Ideas That Took a Decade to Turn a Profit:

ESPN

ESPN was founded by the father-and-son lead team of Bill and Scott Rasmussen in 1978. Most analysts agree that the company did not turn a real profit until 1985.

FEDEX

Frederick W. Smith first had the idea to start FedEX in 1962 while attending Yale University. He was not able to raise the $90 million needed to start the company until 1971. The company did not earn a profit until 1975. It only took Fred Smith 13 years to realize his dream.

FORD MOTOR COMPANY

At just the age of 23 in 1885, Henry Ford saw a gas-powered engine for the first time, and it blew his mind. He began having visions and dreams about creating a "horseless" carriage. Henry obsessed about this idea for 11 years until he was finally able to produce his first automobile in 1896. However, he wasn't financially able to focus on his idea until 1899. In

1901, Henry Ford launched his first auto company, but had to resign later that same year over a financial dispute with bankers (this company is now called Cadillac Motor Car Co.). In 1903, Henry Ford formed the Ford Motor Company and Henry's Model T became the first widely successful and mass-produced automobile in 1908. It only took Henry Ford 23 years to realize his dream.

 TWITTER

Twitter was founded by Jack Dorsey and Jim McKelvey on March 21, 2006. The company did not earn a profit until 2018. It only took Twitter 12 years to earn a profit.

 SQUARE

Square - Square was founded in 2009 by Jack Dorsey and Jim McKelvey (the founders of Twitter) and according to a report published in Inc. Magazine, Square still lost nearly $100 million during 2013. According to most financial data that is available to the public, most experts believe that the company will turn its first profit in 2018. Thus, it will have only taken Square nine years to make a profit.

 GOOGLE

In 1996, Sergey Brin and Larry Page began investing both their time and money into what is now known as Google. Originally, the project was called Backrub with a stated goal of attempting to index and download the entire Internet. In 1999, most humans had never heard of the search engine, and almost no one was using it. However, after several business development deals and five additional years of hard work, Google achieved success and went public in 2004 with a market capitalization of $24 billion.

They became rich quick after investing eight years into building the company.

THE ENTREPRENEUR'S DRAGON ENERGY

 FACEBOOK

One of the world's most popular billionaires is Mark Zuckerberg. Mark became popular as a result of being the fresh-faced billionaire who founded Facebook and became an overnight success.

However, in 2003, before he became an overnight success and a household name, he developed this idea for a website called "Facemash," to try to get his thoughts about his ex-girlfriend out of his mind. Over time, he changed the name of the company to "TheFacebook" and finally to Facebook. In 2005, after over two years spent developing the platform, Facebook reported a $3.63 million loss. But five years later, it finally became the overnight success that many often comment about by saying, "it must be nice."

 AMAZON.COM

Like most entrepreneurs, when Jeff Bezos got the idea to start Amazon. com, he did not simultaneously find the money to turn his dream into reality. Thus, he asked his mom, his dad, and many outside investors to believe in him and his vision. His parents Mike and Jackie invested nearly all of their savings ($300,000) into his business to make it happen. According to Bezos, he gave great deals to the first twenty outside investors who put in an average of $50,000 apiece for a stake of just under 1% of the business. If those early investors would have chosen to hold onto their stakes, they would have been worth $3.5 billion today, which would produce a return of nearly 70,000x.

Three years later, Jeff took his company public and he became an "overnight billionaire." Jeff's initial plan involved him not expecting to make a profit for four to five years.

MICROSOFT

Bill Gates started Microsoft back in beautiful 1975 in an attempt to develop and sell BASIC interpreters designed for the Altair 8800. After six years of working away, he was able to land a contract with IBM to provide their personal computers with their base operating system.

It took another five years until he was able to take Microsoft public in 1986. Thus, after 11 years, he became an overnight success worth $350 million.

 APPLE

It took the now mythological entrepreneur, Steve Jobs, nearly two decades to become an overnight billionaire. He founded the company in his parents' garage in Cupertino, California, in 1976. His company really did not develop any significant traction until it created the Macintosh in 1984, which was eight years later. The company spent the entire 80s and 90s struggling to gain market share, but they finally made it once they invented the iMac and other consumer products. It only took Steve Jobs eight years to "make it big."

 ELEPHANT IN THE ROOM

My brother-in-law and I started the Elephant In The Room Men's Grooming Lounge at 1609 South Boston. The entire team consisted of both he and I working together, and the entire business was funded with our personal cash. To bring in initial customers to "test our system on," we promoted the business directly through my Facebook contacts, Justin's Facebook contacts, and a door-to-door marketing effort that involved him personally walking from business to business passing out "GET A FREE HAIRCUT" cards to people. The homeless community loved those cards, and so did about one out of ten people that we passed those cards out to. Now, store number three in Broken Arrow is thriving, we have now started franchising and have two franchises.

ASK YOURSELF:

» In what way have you not completely sold out and
   burned the boats of retreat to ensure that you will in fact
   obtain your goals?

_____

_____

_____

» Who are the doubters in your camp?

_____

_____

_____

» In what ways are you setting unrealistic expectations for
   the your business or organization rate of growth?

_____

_____

_____

CHAPTER 64

DRAGON ENERGY
POWER PRINCIPLE 64

RECOGNIZE IF SOMEBODY HAS TO BE THE BEST; IT MIGHT AS WELL BE YOU

THE ENTREPRENEUR'S DRAGON ENERGY

NOTABLE QUOTABLE

"People in this world shun people for being great, for being a bright color, for standing out. But the time is now, to be OK with being the greatest you."

- Kanye West

As an entrepreneur, you must obsess about becoming the Greatest Of All Time (GOAT) in your given industry or field. The levels of compensation and satisfaction achieved by top performers are dramatically and exponentially better than those available to the pretenders and intenders. For example, in the field of real estate, there are thousands of real estate agents in Tulsa, Oklahoma, who have licenses, business cards, and their glamour shots on signs, yet the disparity in income between the top producing agents and the average real estate agent is massive. There are thousands of real estate agents in my home town who just like to dress up and play business, but how many real estate agents are truly committed to becoming the best? In the world of music, how many musicians are really sold-out, full-time musicians committed to their craft? How many musicians are just coffee shop weekend warriors who will never take their skill level to the next level because they will never fully commit to what they are doing? What is the difference in the level of compensation and satisfaction enjoyed by Justin Timberlake when he's playing in front of a sold-out arena versus a lazy, yet talented, musician who chooses to play at Whole Foods Market on Sunday mornings?

NOTABLE QUOTABLE

"In our office, to remind our team of the importance of diligence, I have written the following quote above the urinals in the men's restroom, 'When working here your path to success can only be derailed by greed, laziness, half-assness, disorganization, personal problems caused by you and jackassery.'"

- Clay Clark 2017

NOTABLE QUOTABLE

"The Law of Concentration states that whatever you dwell upon grows. The more you think about something, the more it becomes part of your reality."

- Brian Tracy (Canadian-American motivational public speaker and self-development author. He is the author of over seventy books. His popular books are Earn What You're Really Worth, Eat That Frog!, and The Psychology of Achievement.

NOTABLE QUOTABLE

"Move out of your comfort zone. You can only grow if you are willing to feel awkward and uncomfortable when you try something new."

- Brian Tracy

ASK YOURSELF:

» How highly would you rank yourself in your industry? Are you in the top 5% of people who do what you do?

_____

_____

_____

» If you are not in the top 5% of the people in your industry, how can you improve?

_____

_____

_____

» What do you need to improve upon to get into the top 5% of your industry?

_____

_____

CHAPTER 65

DRAGON ENERGY
POWER PRINCIPLE **65**

SET BIG, OVERWHELMING, OPTIMISTIC, MOMENTUM-CREATING GOALS

NOTABLE QUOTABLE

"Get going. Move forward. Aim High. Plan a takeoff. Don't just sit on the runway and hope someone will come along and push the airplane. It simply won't happen. Change your attitude and gain some altitude. Believe me, you'll love it up here."

- President Donald J. Trump

I have literally invested thousands of hours into interviewing billionaires, millionaires, and the world's most successful people, I can tell you that successful people are able to cast a vision that is so real, so big, so profound and inspiring, but at the same time just reachable enough to inspire the minds, actions, and the complete devotion of their team members. However, before you run out there and cast that vision, I believe that it is important to ask yourself the following five tough questions:

ASK YOURSELF:

If we achieve success, what does that really mean? Quantifiably and in terms of metrics, what do you have to do to truly achieve success in your mind?

_____

_____

_____

» Why do you want to achieve these goals?

_____

_____

_____

» What are the specific steps that you and your team must take to achieve these goals?

_____

_____

» What will be the biggest challenges and obstacles standing in your team's way en route to achieving these goals?

_____

_____

_____

» What are the rudest and most difficult questions that people will ask you before they decide to commit years of their life to helping you to achieve this dream?

_____

_____

_____

NOTABLE QUOTABLE

"Where there is no vision, the people perish: but he that keepeth the law, happy is he."

- Proverbs 29:18

CHAPTER 66

DRAGON ENERGY
POWER PRINCIPLE **66**

ACCEPT THAT SIMPLICITY SCALES AND COMPLEXITY FAILS

THE ENTREPRENEUR'S DRAGON ENERGY

I have watched countless small business owners and entrepreneurs fall victim to the belief that "the next idea of the week" will save them. They become conference junkies, sacrificial seminar attending servants, and new idea neophiles who are never able to develop any semblance of traction or success. My friend, if you are going to dominate and achieve both time and financial freedom as an entrepreneur, you must accept that simplicity scales and complexity fails. You must simply embrace the reality that you will achieve success faster once you can solve a problem perfectly one time, and then scale your results millions of times without the involvement of your personal effort.

However, you must also embrace the reality that GET RICH QUICK seminars and GET RICH QUICK charlatans make their money by convincing you that there is a new "GAME CHANGING EVENT, SYSTEM, AND PROCESS that you simply cannot miss out on." My friend, you must resist the addiction to "new ideas." You must simply learn to quiet your mind and learn how to diligently execute proven systems and processes over and over again until you get rich.

NOTABLE QUOTABLE

"In the future, the great division will be between those who have trained themselves to handle these complexities and those who are overwhelmed by them—those who can acquire skills and discipline their minds and those who are irrevocably distracted by all the media around them and can never focus enough to learn."

- Robert Greene

ASK YOURSELF:

» In what ways has your business plan become too complex?

_____

_____

» In what ways has your overall approach to business become too complex to execute?

_____

_____

» In what ways are you allowing yourself to be perpetually distracted as an entrepreneur (new ideas, new business ventures, mindless networking events, serving on bureaucratic and non-action focused boards, etc)?

_____

_____

» How could you DRAMATICALLY simplify your business processes to make them more scalable?

_____

_____

CHAPTER 67

DRAGON ENERGY POWER PRINCIPLE 67

BE COMFORTABLE WITH HAVING GOALS OF YOUR OWN

THE ENTREPRENEUR'S DRAGON ENERGY

NOTABLE QUOTABLE

"I don't care about having a legacy, I don't care about being remembered. The most important thing to me is, while we're here, while we're having fun, while we're sleeping, breathing oxygen, living life, falling in love, having pain and having joy...what can we do with our voice to make things easier, to help someone to make it better for our kids."

- Kanye West

Throughout my career as an entrepreneur and business coach, I've met and personally coached hundreds of business owners who were not happy with the way their lives were going, even though they had been living that way for over 30 years. My friend, super successful people and people who have "Dragon Energy" are very comfortable with setting goals that many people don't agree with, and or that are not embraced by society or viewed as being the cultural norm.

To provide some ample examples, I have listed goals that are 100% my own and not embraced or endorsed by society at large:

– I wanted to have five kids (and we do have five kids).

FUN FACT:

According to the United States Census Bureau, the average American family is 3.14 people in size. - https://www.census.gov/topics/families/families-and-households.html

– I've had the goal to make sure that my kids do not go to college unless it's to gain a specific skill set required for a specific career (lawyer, doctor, etc).

FUN FACT:

"College tuition and fees increased by 'a whopping 1,120%' from 1978 to 2014. At the same time, the price of food rose from 244% and medical expenses 601%." - https://www.usatoday.com/story/opinion/nation-now/2018/05/13/graduation-time-parent-wonders-if-college-worth-money-column/603641002

– My wife and I had the goal to homeschool our kids.

– Leaving a "legacy" is not a goal of mine. My goal is to leave my wife in a financial position where she is well taken care of.

NOTABLE QUOTABLE

"So what is the difference between someone who willfully indulges in sexual pleasures while ignoring the Bible on moral purity and someone who willfully indulges in the selfish pursuit of more and more material possessions while ignoring the Bible on caring for the poor? The difference is that one involves a social taboo in the church and the other involves the social norm in the church."

—David Platt (The best-selling author of Radical - Taking Back your Faith from the American Dream)

– My goal is to not get involved in the community, but rather to get involved in my kids' lives. Do you want to get involved with your local community, and why or why not?

– My goal is to live behind a wall with the letter "C" on the gate and to own a "staycation" destination including a fully operational recording studio, a billiard table, free-range chickens, turkeys, cats, a pond, a lion fountain, and enough pine trees to 100% block out the view of the entire outside world. What is your goal for your personal utopia?

THE ENTREPRENEUR'S DRAGON ENERGY

NOTABLE QUOTABLE

"Control your own destiny or someone else will."

- *Jack Welch*

My goal is to minimize the amount of time I have to spend with people who are not of my choosing. What is your goal in terms of the friendships and people you choose to spend time with, and why?

NOTABLE QUOTABLE

"The secret of happiness is minimizing the amount of time you spent with people you don't choose to be with. This is just math!"

—*Phil Libin*

CHAPTER 68

DRAGON ENERGY POWER PRINCIPLE 68

AVOID OVER-EDUCATED IDIOTS

THE ENTREPRENEUR'S DRAGON ENERGY

From my personal experience, there is a unique group of people who I will define as "educated idiots" these people seem to know vast amounts of theoretical information, but who don't have the tenacity, the mental capacity, or "Dragon Energy" needed to ever turn their brilliant observations and "genius" business ideas into reality. If you want to turn your dreams into reality, it is super important to avoid over-educated idiots.

ASK YOURSELF:

» Who in your life knows the most, but has accomplished the least?

_____

_____

» Who do you know has multiple degrees, but has not ever started a successful business?

_____

_____

CHAPTER 69

DRAGON ENERGY
POWER PRINCIPLE **69**

SCHEDULE YOUR PRIORITIES INTO YOUR CALENDAR

THE ENTREPRENEUR'S DRAGON ENERGY

"Now let's go, take 'em back to the plan

Me and my momma hopped in that U-haul van

Any Pessimists I ain't talk to them

Plus I ain't have no phone in my apartment."

- "Touch the Sky" by Kanye West

NOTABLE QUOTABLE

"Where there is no vision, the people perish: but he that keepeth the law, he is happy."

- Proverbs 29:18

Over time you will observe that no one wants to be lead by someone who has no idea where they are going. It doesn't matter if you are a manager, boss, leader or spouse, you must be one of the rare individuals on planet earth who has goals written down for your life in the areas of:

Faith | Family | Finances | Fitness | Friendship | Fun

On the Thrivetime Show podcasts and in our in-person workshops we refer to these areas of your life and goal setting as the "F6 Life." I would encourage you today to take the time needed write down your goals in the areas of faith, family, finances, fitness, friendship and fun for the next 12 months. Then I would encourage you to the achievement of your goal.

NOTABLE QUOTABLE

"What gets scheduled gets done."

- Lee Cockerell

ASK YOURSELF:

» What are your faith goals for the next 12 months?

_____

_____

» When specifically will you spend time focusing on your faith?

_____

_____

» What are your family goals for the next 12 months?

_____

_____

» When specifically will you spend time each day focusing on your family?

_____

_____

» What are your fitness goals for the next 12 months?

_____

_____

» When specifically will you spend time focusing on your fitness?

_____

_____

» What are your friendship goals for the next 12 months?

_____

_____

» When specifically will you spend time focusing on your friendship?

_____

_____

» What are your financial goals for the next 12 months?

_____

_____

» When specifically will you spend time focusing on your finances?

_____

_____

» What are your goals for fun for the next 12 months?

_____

_____

» When specifically will you spend time focusing on your fun?

_____

_____

» What areass of your business do you plan on improving over the next 12 months?

_____

_____

» What is your overall vision for the direction of the company over the next 12 months?

_____

_____

CHAPTER 70

DRAGON ENERGY
POWER PRINCIPLE 70

DON'T LISTEN TO 99% OF PEOPLE

THE ENTREPRENEUR'S DRAGON ENERGY

ASK YOURSELF:

» What individuals should you allow to provide mentorship and advice in your life?

_____

_____

» What audio podcasts should you listen to in order to fill your mind with the thoughts of super successful people?

_____

_____

» Which individuals should you stop receiving advice from?

_____

_____

CHAPTER 71

DRAGON ENERGY POWER PRINCIPLE 71

BE SELF-SUFFICIENT; DON'T LOOK FOR THE GOVERNMENT TO HELP YOU

THE ENTREPRENEUR'S DRAGON ENERGY

I have yet to meet consistently successful business owners and entrepreneurs who believe in the concept of turning to the government for help with their small business. If you have a created a business plan that calls for heavy government engagement and funding then you should reconsider your methods.

President Ronald Reagan once famously said, "The nine most terrifying words in the English language are, "I'm from the government to come here and help." My Friend, if I had waited on the government grant to start my business, I would still be poor and still be waiting. It doesn't matter whether you are a school seeking to raise funding to support your band program or somebody living in the direct path of an impending hurricane; it is NEVER wise to wait for the government to help you.

Super successful people and people with the game-changing "Dragon Energy" have learned to focus on what they can control to get things done. The poverty mindset teaches you to blame your current circumstances on the economy, the government, or some massive and ambiguous cultural problem that you can't change. YOU MUST LEARN TO FOCUS ON WHAT YOU CAN CONTROL IF YOU WANT TO ACHIEVE SUPER SUCCESS.

NOTABLE QUOTABLE

"Your grammar is a reflection of your image. Good or bad, you have made an impression. And like all impressions, you are in total control."

- Jeffrey Gitomer (The New York Times best-author of Sales Manifesto)

ASK YOURSELF:

» In what ways have you looked to the government to support you and your business ideas over the past five years?

_____

_____

» In what ways could you shift or pivot your existing business plan to be the least reliant on government contracts?

_____

_____

CHAPTER 72

DRAGON ENERGY
POWER PRINCIPLE **72**

DON'T SPEND YOUR DAYS WATCHING TV AND UPDATING SOCIAL MEDIA; CREATE A LIFE PEOPLE WANT TO WATCH ON TV AND SOCIAL MEDIA

THE ENTREPRENEUR'S DRAGON ENERGY

People today love watching TV and updating their social media, The average American according to USA Today is now watching approximately 5 hours of TV per day and spending 2.3 hours per day on their smartphones. This inludes with text messages, social media, and other things that don't matter. My friend, if you want to succeed as an entrepreneur, you must create the seven hours of free time that you need today avoiding your TV and by disengaging with social media altogether. It's sad, but so many people are physically going to work, but are never mentally present because they are constantly distracted by unwanted notification pertaining to people, ideas, and concepts unrelated to their goals. Never underestimate the importance of being mentally and physically present.

FUN FACTS:

» The Average American Watches Over Five Hours of TV Per Day. "On average, American adults are watching five hours and four minutes of television per day. The bulk of that—about four and a half hours of it—is live television, which is television watched when originally broadcast. Thirty minutes more comes via DVR." - "How Much Do We Love TV? Let Us Count the Ways" by John Koblin, The New York Times

» Your Smartphone is Making You Dumb - "Studies indicate that even brief interruptions exponentially increase our chances of making mistakes. This is because when our attention is diverted, we use up valuable cognitive resources reorienting ourselves, leaving less mental energy for completing our work. Research also suggests that frequent decision-making causes us to tire."—Ron Friedman, Ph.D - https://www.psychologytoday.com/us/blog/glue/201501/is-your-smartphone-making-you-dumb

» Your Smartphone is Destroying Your Life - "Here's another disturbing stat: This tally seems to increase daily, but by one study's count, the typical smartphone user interacts with their phone around 85 times per day. And this often includes middle-of-the-night checks for work emails and new 'likes.'" - https://www.psychologytoday.com/us/blog/startup-your-life/201801/why-your-smartphone-is-destroying-your-life

ASK YOURSELF:

» What are you willing to give up to create the life and lifestyle that you want to live (TV, social media, etc)?

_____

_____

_____

» "FOMO," which means the "fear of missing out" is prevelant in todays social media driven culture. What are you prepared to miss out on in order to achieve your goals?

_____

_____

_____

CHAPTER 73

DRAGON ENERGY POWER PRINCIPLE 73

LEARN FROM SETBACKS, DON'T LAMENT ABOUT THEM

NOTABLE QUOTABLE

"I try to learn from the past, but I plan for the future by focusing exclusively on the present. That's where the fun is."

- President Donald J. Trump

If you are going to be an entrepreneur you are going to experience failure and rejection on a daily if not an hourly basis, but you must keep moving. When a bank denies you for the loan that you need, you must be ready to pitch to another bank and to all of the banks if needed. When an investor tells you that they don't like your idea, you have to keep pressing on and find another investor to pitch to. When you make a sales call and get hung up on, you must keep dialing and smiling. When a client is dissatisfied with your service or product you have to just keep going. It's healthy and important that you take the time out to quickly learn from your losses and setbacks, but you simply cannot get into the habit of lamenting over them they are inevitable as a entrepreneur.

DEFINITION: LAMENT
TO EXPRESS SORROW, MOURNING, OR REGRET FOR OFTEN DEMONSTRATIVELY.

You must learn to view every set back as a setup and every adversity as a stepping stone to your ultimate destination and victory, if you are going to win. You must learn to view rejections as that "mean yet oddly effective" coach, teacher or mentor that we all had during school taught us the most.

ASK YOURSELF:

> » In what ways have you been spending too much time lamenting over past disappointments?

_____

_____

> » When your next big adversity smacks you in the face with rejection and disappointment, how long will you allow yourself to be sidetracked emotionally?

_____

_____

CHAPTER 74

DRAGON ENERGY
POWER PRINCIPLE 74

COMMIT OR QUIT BEFORE YOU START

THE ENTREPRENEUR'S DRAGON ENERGY

All successful entrepreneurs have found a way to be "all-in" and 100% committed to their ideas while most people simply view their jobs and every entrepreneurial endeavor as a something that they will invest time and money into to "see if it works." All of the billionaire and millionaire entrepreneurs who I met over the years are committed to their vision, to their workplace, and to their business in a way that is almost religious. There is a massive difference between committing to your spouse 100% of the time and "trying it out to see if it works." There is a HUGE difference between committing to your business idea and "trying it out to see if it works."

ASK YOURSELF:

» Are you 100% committed to your business idea?

_____

_____

» What business venture are you involved in that you are not 100% committed to?

_____

_____

» What is a business concept or idea that you could 100% commit to?

_____

_____

CHAPTER 75

DRAGON ENERGY POWER PRINCIPLE 75

SKY'S THE LIMIT (NOT THE OPINIONS OF OTHER PEOPLE)

THE ENTREPRENEUR'S DRAGON ENERGY

If you want to achieve success in this world, you must not wait for somebody to give you "approval" or to tell you that you have been "chosen" to have success. My friend, history will always favor the bold and those who act as though they have been somehow chosen to do big things. As for me, I don't know where my delusions of grandeur come from, but I have always believed that I have been on a "mission." Every top entrepreneur that I have interviewed has shared similar feelings.

The word "vocation" comes from the latin word vocatio which originally meant, "a call" or "summons." I sincerely believe that all of the successful people that I have ever met act with a sense of purpose—almost as if they have been called to do their job. Meanwhile, everybody else seems to just work as though they are wondering when they can expect their next vacation. When you are working as though you are on a mission, your level of passion, enthusiasm, and focus is exponentially higher than that of the people around you who are working as though they are working for their next escape.

ASK YOURSELF:

» How can you tap into your life's mission with a greater
  sense of urgency and passion?

_____

_____

» What truly motivates you?

_____

_____

» What is your true, 100% authentic vocation?

_____

_____

CHAPTER 76

DRAGON ENERGY
POWER PRINCIPLE **76**

YOUR NETWORK IS YOUR NET WORTH

THE ENTREPRENEUR'S DRAGON ENERGY

NOTABLE QUOTABLE

"It's next to impossible to build a successful business without relationships."

- President Donald J. Trump

Regardless of whether it is a popular, or politically correct thing to write or not, the people around you will absolutely impact your life either positively or negatively. If you choose to surround yourself with people who have never achieved success or who have no desire to make the sacrifices and the tradeoffs needed to achieve success, then you will lose before you start. On a daily basis, I intentionally only interact with successful people. I remember how difficult it was to even engage in basic conversations with friends and family who did not care about achieving success, they were genuinely offended by "Dragon Energy."

NOTABLE QUOTABLE

"It's better to hang out with people better than you. Pick out associates whose behavior is better than yours and you'll drift in that direction."

- Warren Buffett

(How does this tie in with the principle?)

If you want to take your life to the next level this year, I would encourage you to do whatever it takes to begin hanging out and working with people that are doing better than you in the game of life and business. However, it will require you to leave the people that have been holding you back. You will have to leave The Voice watch parties, the social media gossip, and the time-wasting organizations that most people belong to. My friend, are you willing to leave your old ways and old people behind to pursue a new, brighter, better, higher paying, and more satisfying future? Or are you content with hanging out with the masses?

I can vividly remember engaging in conversations with family and friends about my vision to grow DJConnection.com into a national powerhouse. All I heard was negative, feelings-focused feedback from the doubters that I was investing my time with. Now, as I grow The Thrivetime Show Podcast and The Elephant In The Room Men's Grooming Lounge Franchise, I hear nothing but positive feedback, encouragement and motivating mentorship from those around me. Do you know why that is? It's because I have intentionally decided to cut all of the idiots and negative people out of my life.

Too many people choose to become victims when they could, simply choose to become victors. As a kid, I was picked on because I stuttered, our family struggled financially, I had to take both my ACT and Algebra class three times to score a passing grade, and I was sexually abused. But I have never let these events stop me or become excuses for me. Why? My friend, we can all choose to become either victims or victors, and the decision is 100% up to us.

According to hip hop legend, on October 23, 2002, Kanye left a Los Angeles studio after grinding out another late-night session when his rented Lexus collided with another car and left him hospitalized with a fractured jaw. Apparently, this accident was significant enough that it inspired Kanye West to finally make the jump from being a behind-the-scenes producer to becoming an actual rap artist. The first step that Kanye West took en route to becoming a Grammy award-winning rap artist was recording "Through the Wire" while his jaw was still literally wired shut. In the song, he does sound physically strained as though he's in actual pain while rapping each lyric.

THE ENTREPRENEUR'S DRAGON ENERGY

FUN FACT:

"I drink a Boost for breakfast, an Ensure for dessert

Somebody ordered pancakes, I just sip the sizzurp

That right there could drive a sane man berserk

Not to worry, Mr. H-to-the-Izzo's back to wi-zerk

How do you console my mom or give her light support

Telling her her son's on life support?

And just imagine how my girl feel

On the plane, scared as hell that her
guy look like Emmett Till

She was with me before the deal,
she been trying to be mine

She a Delta, so she been throwing that Dynasty sign

No use in me tryin to be lyin', I been trying to be signed

Trying to be a millionaire, how I used two lifelines."

- Kanye West - "Through the Wire"

Throughout my career as a business owner, it honestly has made me laugh out loud multiple times when I have fired somebody for their laziness, and they turned to GoFundMe.com as their backup plan. If you or I get fired, we should ask ourselves what we did to deserve being fired. Great companies don't become great as a result of firing their top employees. Yet, in our culture today, many people are actually turning "being fired" into a cause that is worth being funded and subsidized by other people.

ASK YOURSELF:

» Who are the negative people in your life that need to be cut out?

_____

_____

» What are the negative influences in your life that you must part ways with to go and grow to the next level?

_____

_____

» Who do you need to start spending more time with to grow your life and family to the next level?

_____

_____

» Who do you need to start spending more time with in order to get where you want to go?

_____

_____

» What books do you need to start reading to feed your mind the positivity and mentorship you need to reach the next level?

_____

_____

» How highly would you rank the overall positivity of the people that you have chosen to spend your time with on a scale of 1 to 10, with 10 being the highest, and why?

_____

_____

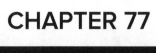

CHAPTER 77

DRAGON ENERGY
POWER PRINCIPLE **77**

IT'S NOT ABOUT RESOURCES; IT'S ABOUT RESOURCEFULNESS

THE ENTREPRENEUR'S DRAGON ENERGY

The United States is a country built on the collective work ethic, aspirations, and dedication of first-generation immigrants who worked as though their lives depended on it, and as though they had no backup plan . . . because they didn't have a backup plan. Too often, I see wannabe entrepreneurs working as though "they have something to lose," They have the mindset that they are entitled to getting "paid sick days" and "paid time off" while they are starting a business. Every successful entrepreneur that I have interviewed either laughs or almost laughs when I ask them about how many days they took off when they were starting their first business, as though I were asking them a trick question. My friend, how you feel is not related to what you must do. You SIMPLY can't get anything done if you only work on the days you feel good. Every time I feel sick, I tend to offer myself a nice, warm glass of "shut-the-heck-up" and then I get back to work.

My friend, if you want to achieve success at the next level, you must become a resourceful grinder who simply refuses to lose on a daily basis. You must become the kind of person who refuses to hit the snooze button each morning when your alarm goes off each day, and become a person who is hell-bent on getting the very most out of each and every resource that you have at your disposal.

George Washington Carver was born a slave, yet he went on to totally revolutionize the way African Americans farmed by developing incredible, new methods to return nutrients to the depleted soil that had been used to plant cotton for years. He developed a new cash crop for his people by inventing hundreds of uses for the peanut. Oprah Winfrey was raped by a family member and had a miscarriage at just the age of 14, yet she has gone on to achieve massive success. Elon Musk was beat up continually as a kid, yet he has gone on to change the world around us by developing PayPal, SpaceX, SolarCity and Tesla. Walt Disney lost it all twice en route to building his Disney empire, yet he did not stop. Thomas Edison and his team recorded over 10,000 failed experiments in their journals and logs before finally creating the first modern, practical light bulb. Andrew Carnegie had to start working at the age of 13 to support his family, yet he overcame. All of the people listed had to overcome, some struggle, and some circumstance en route to achieving their ultimate success. My friend, the choice is up to you. Will you become a victim or a victor?

ASK YOURSELF:

» What resources or talents have you not fully used and taken advantage of?

_____

_____

» In what ways have you been working as though you are entitled to "paid days off" and "paid time off" as an entrepreneur?

_____

_____

THE ENTREPRENEUR'S DRAGON ENERGY

» When have you been the most resourceful thus far as a human on planet Earth, and why?

_____

_____

» When have you been the weakest and most wasteful as a human?

_____

_____

» In what areas of your life have you chosen to be a victim up until now?

_____

_____

» In what areas of your life have you made excuses for yourself up until now?

_____

_____

» In what areas of your life do you need to toughen up and to start overcoming, rather than justifying, mediocre results?

_____

_____

CHAPTER 78

DRAGON ENERGY
POWER PRINCIPLE 78

LEAN INTO PRESSURE, DON'T AVOID IT

THE ENTREPRENEUR'S DRAGON ENERGY

When you start a business at first it's all about just managing yourself, which is tough because very few people around you have learned to say "no" to the things that are not getting them closer to their goals. When you start to say "no" to them and the activities that they want you to participate in it creates and emotional gap between you and those people. That gap is not usually not bridgeable in the future. You will find that over time when you say no to people often times people those same will not like you or will not want to be around you anymore because you rejected them, regardless of how nice you are when you say "no." Merely, saying "no" to most people will cause friction in your relationship and heat.

When I first started DJConnection.com, I was attending college at Oral Roberts University and I lived in the men's dorms on the fourth floor of the Ellis Melvin Roberts Hall, known as EMR. When I was attempting to go to bed at 9p.m. so that I could get up at 3a.m. to work on my business, I was literally the only guy on my dormitory floor trying to get to bed early. I decided to not compete in intramural sports so that I could have more time to focus on growing my business, so I was an outlier and one of the few people who realized that my participation in intramural sports was actually serving as a time-sucking obstacle preventing me from using my college years to actually master the practical skills I needed to pay my bills. Objectively, the time that I had spent playing intramural sports, actually prevented me from learning how to master audio production. I eventually learned to say no to the majority, to the masses, and to what "most people were doing" and I learned to say "yes" to my success, which caused much friction with the people whom at the time I called my friends.

Once I learned the importance of carrying a day-timer and actually honoring the schedule that I created for myself, this too created more pressure and additional conflict for most of the people that I previously spent time with during college. I remember vividly going to a Mexican restaurant near our college dorms looking at my watch and realizing that I had to get back to my dorm room in order to finish a song that I was working on editing. I tried to excuse myself tactfully and when I did a certain individual said, "What do you have going on that is so important?"

I told him that I had to get back to my dorm room so that I could finish a song that I was working on and he and a few other guys just laughed. I remember him asking, "Are you getting paid for that or is that just another one of your ridiculous songs that no one listens to?"

Yet again, experienced "heat" from people who did not care about my vision, my future career or the life that I was trying to create for myself. If you are going to be successful in this world, you must learn how to deal with negative feedback, pressure and the conflict from those that don't share your goals.

ASK YOURSELF:

» In what way have you been drifting from your goals in order to avoid the heat and the potential conflict with other people who will not be sympathetic towards your goals?

_____

_____

» In what ways have you been shying away from doing what needs to be done in order to avoid the pressure that comes with aiming for more than "just enough" and focusing on achieving your goals?

_____

_____

CHAPTER 79

DRAGON ENERGY
POWER PRINCIPLE **79**

AVOID THE OPINIONS OF IDIOTS LIKE THE PLAGUE

The reality is that the vast majority of people don't really know much about anything, but everyone can quickly generate opinions about anything. As an example, when I ask people for their opinion of President Donald J. Trump, nearly everybody has an opinion immediately. In fact, if you were to ask the average person on the street about their opinion of Mr. Kanye West, you would find that most people have a strong opinion one way or the other. Why is it so easy for us all to quickly generate strong opinions about people, places, and things that we know so little about? Why is it so hard for us all to reserve judgement about something or somebody until we have invested the time needed to form a solid opinion based upon facts and research?

As you go out there and attempt to dominate the planet with your business, your concept, or your entrepreneurial idea, I would caution you to refrain from sharing your idea with the vast majority of people. I sincerely do not believe that most people are going to give you the feedback you need. In fact, I think that the feedback and opinions of most people will simply waste your time and slow you down. Do I think it's important to gather feedback? Yes. But I would encourage you to only gather feedback from people who have the mental capacity and wisdom needed to help you. Don't ask fat people for fitness tips. Don't ask people who have been divorced multiple times for marital tips and don't ask people who have never achieved success as an entrepreneur for business advice.

My friend, too many people waste their time talking about their feelings, religion, politics, where they will eat or and the news. Thus, they run out of time to actually go out there and turn their dreams into reality. We only have 24 hours in any given day and you must decide where you will invest that time and with whom you shall invest that time.

ASK YOURSELF:

» Who should you ask for business advice?

_____

_____

» Who should you stop asking for business advice?

_____

_____

» What platforms should you stop sharing your business ideas with (Facebook, Instagram, etc)?

_____

_____

» Who should you no longer allow to speak into your life at all because of their negativity, uninformed opinions, and overall lack of discernment about how life works?

_____

_____

CHAPTER 80

DRAGON ENERGY
POWER PRINCIPLE **80**

DON'T WASTE YOUR TIME WITH FORMAL EDUCATION (UNLESS YOU WANT TO LEARN A SKILL THAT REQUIRES ONE—DOCTORS, LAWYERS, ARCHITECTS, ETC)

THE ENTREPRENEUR'S DRAGON ENERGY

"Man I promise, she's so self conscious
She has no idea what she's doing in college
That major that she majored in don't make no money
But she won't drop out, her parents will look at her funny
Now, tell me that ain't insecure
The concept of school seems so secure
Sophomore three years ain't picked a career
She like fuck it, I'll just stay down here and do hair."

- Kanye West - "All Falls Down"

NOTABLE QUOTABLE

"University administrators are the equivalent of subprime
mortgage brokers selling you a story that you should
go into debt massively—that it's not a consumption
decision; it's an investment decision. Actually, no, it's a
bad consumption decision. Most colleges are four-year
parties . . . Education may be the only thing people still
believe in in the United States. To question education is
really dangerous. It is the absolute taboo. It's like telling
the world there's no Santa Claus . . . Parents see kids
moving back home after college and they're thinking,
'Something is not working. This was not part of the deal.'"

*- Peter Thiel (Silicon Valley venture
capitalist, entrepreneur, and author)*

My friends, we must stop trying to hide behind degrees that don't matter.
Each year, more and more people are waking up after earning a degree only
to discover that their college degree is not helping them find their dream
job, and that the vast majority of degrees do not lead to success. If you just
graduated with an MBA or your doctorate in entrepreneurship, I apologize
that you just wasted both copious amounts of time and money, but you did
and now it's time to focus on learning practical skills that will actually help
you to pay the bills.

NOTABLE QUOTABLE

"Never ever hire an MBA; they will ruin your company."

—Peter Thiel

So what are the best ways to earn practical skills that will help you actually pay the bills?

During your time off, intern for somebody who has achieved massive success.

Listen to podcasts taught by super successful people.

Volunteer to work at your dream job for free until you learn the skills needed for the bosses to justify paying you.

Keep applying for jobs and be willing to work for less money than anybody else.

Show up early and stay late at your current job so that you can ask your current boss for permission to "shadow" and learn from them for free.

Watch documentaries about people that you want to be like.

Stop watching TV, and start reading autobiographies written by super successful people.

ASK YOURSELF:

» What skills do you need to learn to take your life and skills to the next level?

» What skills have you learned in formal education that don't matter at all in the world of business?

_____

_____

» What problems do you need to learn how to solve to take your career to the next level (graphic design, coding, photography, etc)?

_____

_____

CHAPTER 81

DRAGON ENERGY
POWER PRINCIPLE 81

ADOPT THE 5 SECOND RULE. DON'T ALLOW SETBACKS TO EMOTIONALLY CONTROL YOU FOR MORE THAN FIVE SECONDS

THE ENTREPRENEUR'S DRAGON ENERGY

When I was first starting DJConnection.com, every time that I got screwed over by an employee, it would bother me for weeks. My friend, I remember the first time that a "friend" of mine started his own company to directly compete with me by stealing our current customers, our systems, and even one of our employees. It really hurt me and I allowed it to make me mad for months. However, now I sincerely don't allow most things to upset me for more than about five seconds because it is simply not worth it, and partly because I am simply being screwed over too often.

In fact, just this past week, I had a person who was the slowest, most negative and poor performing human we've had involved in our companies over the past 10 years file a complaint saying that they were fired because of something that is 100% false. However, because we are in America, they have the right to lie and to make whatever false claim they want to make, and as an American business owner, I get to pay our wonderful attorney (Wes Carter) a large sum of money to fight this human's bogus claims. Now back in the day, this would have upset me to the point that I could not sleep and I certainly could not home written a book, but now it doesn't even bother me at all. Now, when people make false claims about me on the internet via an online review forum, social media, or some other outlet, it's like a BB hitting a battleship. I simply do not allow little things to bother me anymore, and you shouldn't either.

When my son was born blind, it really rocked my mind and messed me up for months. However, when my father passed away from ALS (Lou Gehrig's Disease), I was able to move on within minutes after his funeral because I have so dramatically altered my mindset on how I choose to handle adversity. I now know that bad things happen to good people and that it could always get worse, but I have now chosen to be thankful for the good things that I have in my life as opposed to dwelling on the bad aspects of my life.

NOTABLE QUOTABLE

"Blessed are those who are persecuted because of righteousness, for theirs is the kingdom of heaven."

- Matthew 5:10

My friend, even Jesus was betrayed by two of his twelve Apostles and was actually put to death at just the age of 33 for being "right." You and I must choose to look for the positive aspects of our daily existence and not let negative circumstances and people kill our positivity.

ASK YOURSELF:

» In what areas of your life are you allowing a small issue to fester and steal your joy?

_____

_____

» In what areas of your life are you allowing yourself to remain bitter and upset with a specific human?

_____

_____

» What recent trials and tribulations do you need to get over and get past starting now?

_____

_____

» On average, how long do you allow negative situations and people to steal your joy?

_____

_____

CHAPTER 82

DRAGON ENERGY
POWER PRINCIPLE *82*

HOLD YOURSELF AND OTHERS TO A HIGHER STANDARD

THE ENTREPRENEUR'S DRAGON ENERGY

Whenever you begin to hold yourself to a high standard in any area of your life, it generally begins to irritate people around you even if it is something as small as just changing your diet. If you start dressing to impress on a daily basis and showing up early to all work commitments, it almost freaks people out. When you start doing more than is expected in all work situations, it will downright piss off the mediocre minds all around you.

If you did the same thing that super successful people do every day, don't you think it is logical to believe that you, too, would become more successful? As you begin to develop the habit of holding yourself and others to a higher standard, get ready for the push back, for the hate, and the resentment of others. People will begin to say, "Do you even get paid for that?" They will say, "Why are you sucking up to the boss so much?" It's amazing how much the masses love mediocrity and despise outliers. You will be disliked you if choose to over deliver and go the extra mile to stand out in the cluttered competition of commerce.

However, once you get through the negativity and initial resentment of your friends and family who don't want to move ahead in this game of life, you will begin to earn the respect of those around you. You will begin to earn this thing called a reputation, which is a good thing. In fact, the equation to earn maximum compensation involves adding up your practical education + your reputation, and this will ultimately determine your level of compensation.

NOTABLE QUOTABLE

"Be a yardstick of quality. Some people aren't used to an environment where excellence is expected."

- Steve Jobs

ASK YOURSELF:

» In what ways could you raise your personal standards in terms of appearance?

_____

_____

» In what ways could you raise your standards in terms of work performance?

_____

_____

» In what ways could you improve your standards for work quality?

_____

_____

CHAPTER 83

DRAGON ENERGY POWER PRINCIPLE 83

BE PREPARED TO BE THE ONLY ONE ON THE PLANET WHO BELIEVES IN YOUR DREAMS

THE ENTREPRENEUR'S DRAGON ENERGY

Once you begin to bring the "Dragon Energy" to your daily life, you will quickly discover that most people will simply be unable to keep up with your work ethic and your visions for the future. They are trapped in a world-view that values being liked and accepted, maintaining the status quo, and being loved above all else. To most people, the thought "they could be right" and that everybody else on the planet could be wrong is terrifying and almost too much to handle. Consider these examples:

Socrates was put to death because he was convicted of asebia (impiety) against the pantheon (temple) of Athens and for the corruption of the youth because he failed to acknowledge the gods that the city acknowledged, and he introduced the concept of new deities.

In 1517, Martin Luther penned a document attacking the Catholic Church's corrupt practice of selling "indulgences," which basically granted people forgiveness from sin. Think about this concept: the Catholic Church was actually selling forgiveness in exchange for money. He nailed this document known as the Ninety-Five Theses to the door of the Wittenberg Castle. The Ninety-Five Theses focused on two central beliefs that were "crazy" and "revolutionary" at the time: humans may reach salvation only by their faith and not by their deeds, and the Bible is the central religious authority, not the Catholic Church. On November 9th of 1518, the Pope condemned Luther's writings as conflicting with the teachings of the Church.

In the month of July 1520, Pope Leo X issued a papal bull (essentially a public decree) that concluded that Martin Luther's Ninety-Five Theses were heretical, and he gave him 120 days to recant in Rome. When Luther refused to do so, he was officially excommunicated by the Church on January 3rd of 1521. Essentially, the POPE WAS CONDEMNING MARTIN LUTHER TO HELL BECAUSE HE COMMITTED THE VERY SERIOUS CRIME OF BELIEVING THAT THE CHURCH SHOULDN'T BE SELLING FORGIVENESS.

In 1633 Galileo Galilei, the famous Italian astronomer and physicist, was crazy enough to believe that the Earth was not the center of the Universe. The legal body of the Catholic Church (known as the Inquisition) accused him of heresy, and he was later sentenced to life imprisonment beginning in 1633. Because he was in such bad health, he was allowed to serve out his prison sentence under house arrest for the CRIME OF BELIEVING THAT THAT EARTH WAS NOT THE CENTER OF THE UNIVERSE.

In 1856, Henry Bessemer took out a patent on what became known as the "Bessemer Process," which became the modern process used to mass-produce and manufacturer steel. Many people at the time thought that Bessemer was a witch doctor because he was one of the first people able to remove the impurities from the iron by oxidation as a result of air being blown through the molten iron.

In 1922, Mohandas Gandhi was sent to prison for organizing civil disobedience after a protest march turned violent and ultimately resulted in the death of 22 people. Gandhi was the man who led the Indians in pushing back against the British-imposed rule, and did not stop until he was ultimately assassinated in 1948 by a British nationalist.

Beginning in 1954, Reverend Martin Luther King Jr. became the most prominent and well-known leader of the civil rights movement until the time of his assassination in 1968. His CONTROVERSIAL BELIEF was best summarized when he once famously said, "I have a dream that my four little children will one day live in a nation where they will not be judged by the color of their skin, but by the content of their character." Isn't it amazing that just 60 years ago in the United States of America, a man and his family had to live under the constant fear of violence and death simply because he wanted people of color to be judged based upon the content of their character and not the color of their skin?

On December 1st of 1955, Rosa Parks boarded a bus in Alabama after a long day of work to head home. During the bus ride, the bus driver asked her to give up her seat for a caucasian passenger, but she refused and was arrested for disobeying Alabama's ridiculous and racist law. Her arrest ultimately led to a 381-day long boycott of the entire Montgomery Alabama bus system and the 1956 Supreme Court Decision to ban segregation on the public transportation system.

From 1981 to 2001, Jack Welch served as the CEO of GE and despite being controversial for his management philosophy known as "differentiation," Welch was able to grow the company by 4,000% during his tenure. His controversial management method involved being transparent with employees and rating everyone within the company by giving them a letter grade A, B, or C rating based on their work performance.

NOTABLE QUOTABLE

"If there is one of my values that pushes buttons, it is differentiation. Some people love the idea; they swear by it, run their companies with it, and will tell you it is at the very root of their success. Other people hate it. They call it mean, harsh, impractical, demotivating, political, unfair—or all of the above. Obviously, I am a huge fan of differentiation. I have seen it transform companies from mediocre to outstanding, and it is as morally sound as a management system can be. It works. Companies win when their managers make a clear and meaningful distinction between top- and bottom-performing businesses and people, when they cultivate the strong and cull the weak."

—Jack Welch

In 1999, Shawn Fanning introduced the peer-to-peer file sharing program known as Napster to the world. Napster spread like wildfire, and Shawn was actually featured on the cover of Time Magazine. Many thought the file sharing program would kill the music industry, however as of 2018, online digital music streaming services such as Pandora, Spotify, and iTunes are creating a platform for new independent artists to be discovered.

ASK YOURSELF:

» In what areas of your life have you allowed yourself to be pushed over by family and friends just to keep the peace?

_____

_____

» In what areas of your life should you begin to stand up for yourself even it means irritating people that you've known for years or organizations that you have been a part of for a long-time?

_____

_____

CHAPTER 84

DRAGON ENERGY POWER PRINCIPLE **84**

YOUR COMPENSATION IS BASED ON YOUR PRACTICAL EDUCATION, YOUR REPUTATION, AND YOUR ABILITY TO INFLUENCE PEOPLE THROUGH CONVERSATION

In our culture today, there are way too many college graduates living in their parent's home and complaining about how their college degree is not helping them earn their dream job. You and I both have met hundreds of people who have earned completely worthless degrees that never taught them a skill that can be used to pay the bills. If that is you, you must get over it. So you threw $60,000 and four years of your life away. I get it. Get over it.

Just two weeks ago, I met somebody in their 40s who had been a school teacher since the age of 22 and was so frustrated that their multiple degrees had not earned them higher wages. Well my friend, this just in . . . Our society values professional athletes more than professional teachers. People wait in line for hours to see a Justin Timberlake concert and to buy replica jerseys to wear while cheering for their favorite players during NBA games, but people do not wait in line to cheer for their favorite public school teachers. People don't buy jerseys to dress up like their favorite math teacher. In fact, the vast majority of people can't even remember the names of most of their teachers. If you are reading this and you have found yourself at a place in life where you are frustrated by the lack of compensation that you are making, then it's time to make a change. Take a moment to answer the following questions:

ASK YOURSELF:

» What are problems that you can solve that humans are actually willing to pay to have solved?

_____

_____

» What are problems that you would be interested in learning to solve that humans would actually be willing to pay to have solved (coding, photography, baking, automotive repair, home remodeling, etc)?

_____

_____

NOTABLE QUOTABLE

"THERE are two kinds of knowledge. One is general, the other is specialized. General knowledge, no matter how great in quantity or variety it may be, is of but little use in the accumulation of money. The faculties of the great universities possess, in the aggregate, practically every form of general knowledge known to civilization. Most of the professors have but little or no money. They specialize on teaching knowledge, but they do not specialize on the organization or the use of knowledge."

—Napoleon Hill

ASK YOURSELF:

» What are practical skills that you need to learn this year to take your life and income to the next level?

_____

_____

» What are things that you learned in college that are 100% not applicable to your daily life?

_____

_____

» What classes did you take in college that were the biggest waste of time?

_____

_____

» How much did you actually pay per accredited hour for college?

_____

_____

» How much would you be willing to pay to learn an actual, practical skill that would give you the ability to pay your bills?

_____

_____

As an entrepreneur, you will get paid based on what you do, not based on what you intend to do. You must accept the fact that your ideas and intentions don't matter at all. Our world will only pay you based on the value that you bring to your hours, not for the hours that you put into something.

CHAPTER 85

DRAGON ENERGY POWER PRINCIPLE 85

ACCEPT AND EMBRACE THAT HISTORY FAVORS THE BOLD

THE ENTREPRENEUR'S DRAGON ENERGY

When I started DJConnection.com out of my college dorm room, nobody encouraged me. When I say NOBODY, I sincerely mean that NOBODY encouraged me to start that business. When I had the game plan to call up the largest companies in Tulsa to offer them to allow me to provide disc jockey, party planning, and entertainment services for just $1 for their first show, EVERYBODY thought I had lost my mind. Once I received the Tulsa Metro Chamber Young Entrepreneur of the Year Award in 2002, people called me to tell me congratulations.

When I had the vision to expand the business into multiple cities such as Dallas, Texas and Kansas City, Missouri, NOBODY (other than my wife) who worked with me at the time believed that it was possible. EVERYBODY (other than my wife) told me that brides and event planners had to meet their disc jockeys first before they would feel comfortable with booking. However, in 2007, when I won the United States Entrepreneur of the Year Award for the State of Oklahoma, people called me and told me congratulations.

When my brother-in-law and I teamed up to start The Elephant In The Room Men's Grooming Lounge in an attempt to take the standard of men's grooming to the next level, nobody believed in us. I did not care and I still don't care. If you want to take your life to the next level, then you are going to have to learn how to develop the courage and conviction needed to go out there and turn your dreams into reality when nobody else believes in you. In fact, I would caution you that if everybody believes your idea is great, then that might just mean that you are 100% wrong because the vast majority of people don't know what they are talking about, and I sincerely believe that.

In fact, next time you go to ask someone for their opinion or the next time you find yourself listening to the unsolicited opinions of family, friends, acquaintances, and popular culture at large, consider this:

FUN FACTS:

> » 78 percent of the men interviewed had cheated on their current partner.

—*"5 Myths About Cheating" — https://www. washingtonpost.com/opinions/five-myths-about-cheating/2012/02/08/gIQANGdaBR_story. html?noredirect=on&utm_term=.05ab54a87466*

"75% of employees steal from the workplace and most do so repeatedly." — https://www.cbsnews. com/news/employee-theft-are-you-blind-to-it

"9.4 percent of the population—had used an illicit drug in the past month." — https://www.drugabuse. gov/publications/drugfacts/nationwide-trends

"4 to 6 million people, would be considered problem gamblers, people whose gambling affects their everyday lives." — https://www.livestrong. com/article/119442-gambling-addiction-stats

"The average American watches five hours of TV per day." — https://www.nytimes.com/2016/07/01/ business/media/nielsen-survey-media-viewing.html

"One in eight American adults is an alcoholic." — https://www.washingtonpost.com/news/wonk/ wp/2017/08/11/study-one-in-eight-american-adults-are-alcoholics/?utm_term=.92dda665f4b9

THE ENTREPRENEUR'S DRAGON ENERGY

My friend, fortunately for you, most people don't have the "Dragon Energy." Most people are not myopically focused on achieving success in the areas of their faith, family, finances, fitness, friendship and fun, and thus they are easy to beat in the competition of commerce. I mean, it's not even fair. If you are competing with someone who doesn't wake up until 8a.m. everyday and who skips work any time they don't feel like working, you are going to destroy them because people with the "Dragon Energy" have been up since 5a.m. planning their day and making things happen. This means that you have a 3-hour head start against your competition every day. And whether we are talking about running a marathon or competing in the world of business, getting a daily 3-hour head start ahead of your competition is incredible for you, and not so good for them.

However, most people that you know don't have the "Dragon Energy" that you now have, but they make up for their lack of success by having 10 times as many opinions about everything than the people at the top. The people at the bottom love throwing rocks at Kanye West, President Donald Trump, John D. Rockefeller, Michael Jordan, Andrew Carnegie, Oprah Winfrey, and people who have gone on to have massive success because they are busy enough pursuing their own goals.

NOTABLE QUOTABLE

"Courage is not the absence of fear. Courage is the ability to act effectively, in spite of fear."

- President Donald J. Trump

ASK YOURSELF:

» What do you fear the most about leaving the masses behind?

_____

_____

» Who is the most perpetually negative person in your life that you fear leaving the most?

_____

_____

» What difficult conversations do you fear having the most that are holding you back?

_____

_____

» What is the biggest, time-wasting activity in your life that you worry about giving up the most?

_____

_____

CHAPTER 86

DRAGON ENERGY POWER PRINCIPLE 86

HE WHO HAS THE MOST OPTIONS WINS | THE RULE OF 3

THE ENTREPRENEUR'S DRAGON ENERGY

People with "Dragon Energy" have recognized that the person with the most options almost always wins. You must always have at least 3 options: 3 potential employees, 3 potential vendors and 3 potential babysitters lined up for all situations in which you expect and demand excellence. If you have ever had kids and have ever worked with babysitters, you will quickly recognize the truth of what I am writing here. All babysitters could be divided into three categories:

The Boyfriend Crazy Babysitter: The boyfriend crazy babysitter is a person who is 100% interested in watching your kids until they have a potential dating opportunity arise. When they have a potential dating opportunity arise, they will give you a professional "30 minute notice" to find another babysitter. This is why you must have multiple babysitter options ready to go if you are serious about going on an actual date and you have five kids (like my wife and I do).

The Ransom Babysitter: This human is somebody who will be the best babysitter on the planet until they discover that they can get paid more to watch somebody else's kids. Once they discover that there is a better opportunity, regardless of how much you are paying this person, they will typically give you a one-week opportunity to meet their pay demands or they will ghost you for another family. This is another reason you must have multiple babysitter options ready to go if you are serious about going on an actual date.

The I'm-Sorry-For-The-Late-Notice-But Babysitter: This personality type loves to start off their outbound, last minute phone call to you by saying, "I'm sorry for the late notice, but . . ." and then essentially bail on you one out of every three weeks you schedule them.

However, this is why you must have multiple babysitter options ready to go if you are serious about EVER going on an actual date.

People with "Dragon Energy" have learned that we simply cannot afford to trust people based on what they say they are going to do, but rather we must learn to judge people based on what they actually do. I don't care what religious background you have or what motivational books you have been reading lately about "how great leaders can inspire everyone," you must embrace the reality of this concept, or you will lose. I can honestly say that embracing the harsh reality of how people really are, versus believing in what people say they are, is one of the biggest differences successful people and underachievers. People who never achieve super success always "believe the best in people," and people who do achieve super success always "face reality as it is and not as they wish it be."

NOTABLE QUOTABLE

"As I grow older, I pay less attention to what men say. I just watch what they do."

—*Andrew Carnegie*

ASK YOURSELF:

» In what ways have you been setting yourself up for certain failure as a result of planning your life around what people say versus what people actually do?

_____

_____

» Who in your life do you keep falsely believing in simply because you are related to them?

_____

_____

» Who in your business is absolutely killing your reputation and your overall quality of service or product as a result of not doing what they say they are going to do?

_____

_____

» In what ways have you allowed yourself to be perpetually stuck in a doom loop because you are waiting on somebody to do what they say they are going to do?

_____

_____

CHAPTER 87

DRAGON ENERGY
POWER PRINCIPLE 87

TRUST, BUT VERIFY EVERYTHING AND EVERYBODY

THE ENTREPRENEUR'S DRAGON ENERGY

People with "Dragon Energy" do not trust the vast majority of people because they are aware of the harsh reality that most people are unfaithful to their spouse, lie on their resumes, and steal from the workplace. They only allow a very small number of people into their "inner circle," and they speak in vague generalities when in the presence of people that they cannot trust. Because the vast majority of people love engaging in gossip so much, top performers who have "Dragon Energy" will often ask people who want to be close to them to "keep a secret" that doesn't really matter just to see if it gets out to the outside world. My friend, as I have climbed up higher and higher up the ladder of success, it has become more and more clear that VERY FEW people can be trusted, and thus you must proceed with caution whenever you speak with anybody about anything ever.

ASK YOURSELF:

» In what ways have you set yourself up for failure in the past by trusting, but not verifying, what people say?

_____

_____

» In what ways have you been taken advantage of in the past by not verifying what somebody is saying?

_____

_____

> » Why does society think that it is mean, wrong, negative, or pessimistic to operate with the mindset of "trust, but verify"?

_____

_____

As an entrepreneur, you must understand that the vast majority of the world misunderstands what it means to delegate. When you delegate something, the process should look like this:

Assign the action items:

> » Follow up to verify that the action items were done

> » Insist on results and discipline (actually getting things done)

When the vast majority of people think about delegating something, they view the process like this:

> » Assign the action items

> » Assume that the action items were done

When the action items are not done, sympathize with the person who failed to hit their deadline (because of their allergy to gluten, their marital problems, their headache, their forgetfulness, their miscommunication, their pursuit of work-life balance or their baby's daddy, etc)

My friend, my hope is that this book will help you take your personal level of success to the next level. However, before we conclude, I want to caution you with this final word of wisdom before you go out there and diligently execute your plans and turn your dreams into reality. Most people are going to resent your success. Most people simply do not like it when somebody that they know achieves dramatically more success than everybody else, and they will start to openly say things like:

» "Who do they think they are?"

» "Where do they get off thinking that they are better than us?"

» "It looks like they have forgotten where they came from."

When word of their comments, negativity, and gossip gets back to you, you must learn how to train your mind to feed off of their negativity and their "haterade." All of the super successful people that I have had the opportunity to be around actually thrive when they are experiencing hate from all sides, and that is what you must learn to do. You must learn somehow to enjoy their negativity, their side comments, and their jealousy. You must learn how to turn their hate into a fuel, and that fuel is called...

"DRAGON ENERGY."

CPSIA information can be obtained
at www.ICGtesting.com
Printed in the USA
FSHW010631050421
80102FS